Leading in a Changing World

Updated Edition

Leadership Lessons for Future-Focused Leaders

By Graeme Codrington and Keith Coats

2021 Edition

All feedback welcomed on
info@tomorrowtodayglobal.com

ISBN 978-0-6398022-1-3

Preface to the Updated 2020s Edition

By Jude Foulston, *editor*
May 2019

As the editor of both the first edition of *Leading in a Changing World* and now this updated second edition, I thought it would be a good idea (and of interest to you as the reader) to sit down with Keith (KC) and Graeme (GC) to clarify a few things as to what has prompted this second edition.

Before we start with some of the questions I have for you, congratulations on your first edition being a best seller – were you surprised by the market response?

GC: Yes and no. Obviously, as an author, I always hope that my books will sell well. I wish they'd sell millions of copies, and help pay off my house, but I think I've worked out by now that I am no JK Rowling. But, truthfully, way more important than trying to earn a living as an author, for me there is huge gratification in knowing that the information that was in my head translated into words, which have in turn found their way into other people's lives and made a tangible difference to them. The 'best seller' label simply means that enough people thought the book was helpful enough to share it and recommend it to others, and I really like that.

KC: Yes, I agree with what Graeme said. I think our book touches a nerve and offers some simple but practical suggestions as to what it means – and takes – to be 'future fit'. It was a fun experience to collaborate on the first edition and we have enjoyed the second run at it as well.

Let's turn our attention then to this second edition… why the need for a second edition?

KC: Firstly, things have changed since 2015 when we wrote *Leading in a Changing World*. The challenge of what it means to lead in this complex and changing landscape remains, and we thought rather than write an entire new book we could refresh and update our content within the parameters of a title that is forever relevant.

GC: Since writing the first edition, we have been asked to speak about it at company conferences and workshop the contents at numerous leadership development conferences. We've discovered what connects with people, and what was confusing or needed more explanation. We have also learnt from our delegates, and been amazed at their insights, questions, and stories. We wanted to include these.

So what is 'new' in this second edition?

GC: There are three new things in this edition: (1) We have changed the structure of the book, making it more readable; (2) we have added two key new leadership focus areas that have become increasingly important for leaders over the past few years, namely diversity and disruption; and (3) we have significantly updated the five key leadership responses to our invitational model, especially the issue of leadership development. All of these have added a lot more value by bringing practical applications and implications to leaders.

Who is the book's target audience?

KC: Well, leaders – any leader really. And those people who want to – and hope to – be leaders in the future. Hopefully this book will help provide clarity and serve as something of a 'sense-maker' for anyone in a leadership role or position. But I don't think it is limited to people who have formal leadership positions and titles. At one level, we are all leaders. Parents are leaders. Teachers are leaders. Supervisors are leaders. Anyone who influences others is a leader, and this book will help them.

Is this the 'final word'?

KC: Well, if you mean by 'final word' a definitive message on the subject of leading in a changing world... most definitely not! No one really can have the 'final word'. This book is not meant to be a definitive voice on the topic but rather a guide, a conversation starter, a collection of thoughts, frameworks, insights, and questions designed to prompt and assist leaders and individuals in their quest to remain relevant and be fit for whatever tomorrow holds.

That said, I also sincerely hope it is not the 'final word' when it comes to further collaboration with Graeme as far as books go. As we continue our own learning journey, I am sure there will be lots more we could say/write, but I guess that will depend on who is listening!

GC: I agree. This is not even OUR final word on the topic. It does reflect some of the best of our thinking at the moment, but we are always learning and developing and hope to be able to share more in the future by way of new books.

Final question: As founding partners of TomorrowToday, you must take a measure of pride in how far TomorrowToday's reach has extended... tell me what it has been like to share this journey and what's next for you and TomorrowToday.

GC: As we say in the introduction to this book, we used to be quite nervous that we were both business partners and such good friends. But two decades later, we seem to have found a formulae that makes the most of both of those relationships. I am not just proud of what we have done – I have a deep sense of life-fulfilment. Some people ask me when I am going to move on or get a new job, or sound amazed that I am still in the same job after nearly 20 years. But honestly, I don't want to do anything else with my life. Our team has made a significant impact on the lives of so many people. It is a real privilege to do what we do, and to be able to do it so successfully for so long. I wouldn't do anything else. I just want to get even better at doing it! That's what's next for me.

KC: It has been a great journey and one I wouldn't swap for anything. If at the outset, sitting looking out over the Indian Ocean just north of Durban, you had told us that we would have worked in over 100 countries that include Russia, China, Iran, Australia, Japan, Singapore, Brazil, Nigeria, India, Kenya, Iceland, Switzerland, Greece, Cambodia, Estonia, Chile, and the state of Hawaii, well I think our response would have been, 'what are you smoking?' Not only that, but our travel has intersected with top educational institutes such as London Business School, Gordon Institute of Business Science, Duke CE, the East-West Center, Cornell, and Insead, not to mention blue-chip companies including Boeing, Credit Suisse, Rolls Royce, Deutsche Bank, Nestle, Novartis, Deloitte, Barclays, Microsoft, Unilever, Spar, and Sage. Yes, it has been some adventure!

But at our core, we have tried to be a company that not only 'lives our message', but also one that is fundamentally relational. Of course, we have made mistakes and no doubt disappointed people along the way, but I think we have got a lot more 'right' than 'wrong' as we have navigated our way since those early days.

Remember Graeme, our 'mantra'… 'if we build it, they will come', borrowed, of course, from the movie *Field of Dreams*.

GC: And that's where the nerdy research geek in me cannot help myself: that line is never said in *Field of Dreams*. I promise it isn't.

JUDE: And right there is the essence of TomorrowToday that we hope is never lost: deep insights underpinned by great research, but never lost in the details; overlaid with gentle humour, practical wisdom, and a constant sense of wanting to add real value in whatever we do.

It has been a treat updating this book. We hope you enjoy reading it – whether it's for the first time, or whether you are reading it again.

Preface to the 2015 Edition
(We've left this in the new edition, because it is still worth reading!)

There's a rule in Hollywood: never work with children or animals. They're unpredictable and will likely outshine you in key scenes. Luckily there's no such rule against friends or business partners working together on a creative project. It's taken 15 years of friendship and 12 years of partnership in business, but we've finally been able to write a book together.

This book is the culmination of over a decade spent immersed in trying to understand the changing world of work and the implications this has on people. It emerges from the intersection of deep academic study and extensive reading, a global client base that spans every continent and industry, our own personal experiences of leadership and change, and the efforts and insights of our many colleagues and associates at our strategic insights firm, TomorrowToday Global.

We've written this book out of a deep desire to share some of what we've discovered about leading in a changing world through the study, work, and experiences we've had. The leaders we've shared these insights with already – by way of presentations, workshops, leadership development programmes, blogs, online courses, and coaching – have been able to find new ways of navigating the complex world we are now faced with, and have provided invaluable feedback for our models and methods. We know this book is merely a milestone on our shared journey into this new world of work, and we look forward to sharing it with you. Please do connect with us, give us feedback, share your stories, ask your questions, and join us as we create a new future together. We're as keen to learn as we are to share what we've discovered already.

Writing a book together is fun; it is also hard work. Merging individual stories, friendships, and thinking into some coherent stream that is presented in a consistent and sense-making format posed some challenges we didn't anticipate at the outset. So, a small note on style: we have decided to consistently speak from the collective pronoun of 'we', 'our', etc. in sharing our stories and words with you. We have many shared stories, of course, with nearly two decades of shared lives. But our choice in this book is mainly stylistic, making the book easier to read and less confusing as to whose 'voice' is speaking.

There are some exceptions when the integrity of what is being shared dictates differently, but these are rare.

Our thoughts and insights come from a shared journey that precedes the formal start of TomorrowToday Global; they come from a friendship that has always been lived forward, but is best understood and appreciated when looking backwards. Throughout the years, there have been robust conversations and different perspectives, but such edges have always been anchored by a deep respect and a shared sense of destiny in the 'TomorrowToday way'. Many of the suggestions and insights have been drawn from our own experiences, from the good and the bad, from the successes and failures that have marked our remarkable journey in the company we started together in 2002.

Since then, our work has taken us to well over 100 countries, with a combined average of nearly 300 client engagements a year, every year. These clients represent the breadth of human endeavour, from large multinationals to small startups and family businesses; we work with corporates and non-profits, governments and schools. Probably most important is the fact that many of our clients are repeat clients, with CEOs and senior leaders asking us back again and again.

We love what we do, and we love that we get to do it together and as part of a larger team at our firm. And now we get to share it with you.

If you'd like to know more about us and who we are, there are brief bios at the end of this book and links to our websites below. You can also see what our team does at http://www.tomorrowtodayglobal.com. And, of course, you're welcome to contact us. This is a journey worth sharing.

Keith Coats
http://www.keithcoats.com
keith@tomorrowtodayglobal.com
@keithcoats

Graeme Codrington
http://www.graemecodrington.com
graeme@tomorrowtodayglobal.com
@futuristgraeme

May 2015

Table of Contents

Introduction

If the world is changing, leadership needs to change.
The world is changing.
It is that simple; it is that complex.

2020 saw our world changed. Same planet, different world.

Through our work in TomorrowToday Global, we have been at the very forefront of this intersection of a changing world and changing leadership across the broad scope of industries and sectors spanning all corners of the globe, and what we see concerns us.

We see leaders who are frustrated that they can't mobilise their teams to adapt quickly enough to change. We see leaders who feel the horizon of their strategic plans rushing ever closer, resulting in decision-making that often feels closer to guesswork than science. We see leaders battling to manage their teams, to keep and get the most of talent, to develop succession plans, and to ensure everyone is focused on the same outcomes. We see leaders exasperated at the lack of initiative displayed by their teams, and yet equally bound by increasing regulation, bureaucracy, and inertia. We see leaders struggling to come to terms with the implications of a global pandemic and make sense of a forever changed landscape.

We see leaders struggling to lead in a context unlike anything they have ever seen or experienced.

We see leaders unable to admit that they're struggling to lead.

Maybe the symptoms we've just listed don't *all* apply to you, or maybe you have a sense that your organisation's problems lie elsewhere. Whatever the specific issues are, we're sure you'll agree with us that leadership isn't what it used to be. A big part of the reason for this is that leadership itself is changing – just as the world around us has irrevocably changed and of course, will continue to change in dramatic ways.

If nothing else 2020 has exposed deep-seated flaws in how we have built organisations and our preparedness for unexpected disruption. Much of our leadership thinking and practice has been exposed as outdated and unsuitable for the context and reality that surround us. The global pandemic has accentuated and amplified trends that were already in play but largely being ignored: from the realisation that we no longer live in a 'complicated world' but rather a 'complex world' (and what this means) to the radical acceleration of digital transformation. Every aspect of leadership needs to change: leadership theory, leadership practice, leadership measurements, leadership reviews – no aspect of leadership is going to remain unchanged and unexamined in the 2020s and beyond. If there is to be something to take from 2020 it is the realisation of the need to reimagine and reset our approach to leadership and how we build future fit organisations.

The only way to change all this is for leaders (and those tasked with the responsibility of leadership development) to step back, rethink things, and be willing to change. It means asking searching questions, challenging assumptions, and revisiting formulae that have, for a very long time, worked rather well.

This is easier said than done and, thanks to 2020, we have been given our 'wake-up' call!

But it can be done, and this is what our book is about. Future-focused leaders will gain insight into what it takes to succeed in a time of disruptive change. We hope that the book provides both a new lens through which to see the world and leadership, as well as practical tools and tips to help you make the journey towards a new leadership style and approach.

In this book we do not present a single, unified theory of leadership (there isn't one!), nor do we motivate a one-size-fits-all set of leadership practices (although we recommend and suggest a few we've found helpful). We wish it was that easy, but that's actually part of the problem – that leaders seek simple solutions in a time of deepening complexity. Instead, this book is about the issues that leaders need to rethink, and what is required to develop an adaptability that will allow them to lead, to 'do', and to 'be' whatever is required of them.

It's time to change

When you discover you are riding a dead horse, the best strategy is to dismount. Strange as it might seem, we have met many in leadership

who are attempting just that: trying to ride dead horses – and with commendable enthusiasm at that! The fact that the horse is dead, whilst obvious to others, is seemingly lost on them.

It is clear that the character and style of leadership are changing. The irrepressible forces of technology, demographics, institutional and structural changes, together with value shifts, all impact on leadership. In a world where how we organise and go about our business is adapting constantly, leadership that remains fixed and static is rendered obsolete, irrelevant, and, well… dead.

And so, if you find yourself astride a dead horse… the best strategy is to dismount!

Much has been said and written about change and the importance for leaders – wherever they might be – to adapt to the changes that are taking place around them. If those changes bring about deep, structural shifts, then the art and science of leadership itself may have to change. In fact, a new approach to what it means 'to change' might be required, and leadership may need to become far more adaptive in order to be effective.

You'll find a roadmap for doing just that in this book.

On one level, there's nothing new in this thought. Former Chrysler CEO Lee Iacocca wrote in his book *Where Have All the Leaders Gone?* (2008) that 'leadership is all about managing change – whether you are leading a company or leading a country'. Harvard academic and author Barbara Kellerman, in her excellent book *Professionalizing Leadership* (2018), defines a leader as 'an agent of change, for good or bad'. They are right. Jack Welch is credited with saying that 'when the rate of change outside exceeds the rate of change inside, the end is in sight'. The leader's world has always been one that has had to deal

with, adapt to, and ultimately embrace change. Due to the vantage point enjoyed by leaders, it becomes their primary responsibility to recognise, interpret, and respond to the constant change at hand.

What is new now is the era or context in which we live, one characterised by deep, structural changes to the way the world works. Against this constantly moving backdrop, leaders need to intentionally build systematic frameworks that will yield a bigger picture and understanding from which they can then act.

One of the compelling reasons for leaders to engage in this work is that they increasingly find themselves leading in a paradoxical world. Paradox is the 'right-right' clash of values and behaviours. It can be located in the context of a number of familiar situations: structural, generational, cultural, gender specific, technological, and artistic. Of course, paradoxes have always existed. It is just that they now sit closer to the surface, exposed and more acutely experienced than ever before, in a world that is getting ever smaller.

We have encountered many a leader spending time and energy attempting to resolve the paradox he or she is facing. Paradox by its very definition cannot be 'resolved', and this is why it becomes important to be able to both identify and understand the situation faced as paradoxical. Frameworks become the 'sense-making tools' that enable leaders to do this essential work.

A key question for leaders becomes how this accelerating paradox and connectivity at every level will affect what they do and how and where they do it. Certainly it leads to an understanding and appreciation that the changing world impacts on both work (the working environment and how we organise and regulate work) and on the work force (those doing the work) itself. Put another way, the 'rules of the game are changing': the rules for both leadership and what it will take to create a

competitive advantage are changing. This can be very disconcerting for those leaders who are banking on experience to see them through – by which we mean that the answer to the current problem is to be found in yesterday's solution. That wise sage Peter Drucker once said, 'The greatest danger in times of turbulence is not the turbulence, it is to act with yesterday's logic.'

The world is changing. It's time to learn the new rules.

A leadership journey

This book brings together the combined insights of Keith Coats and Graeme Codrington, two of the co-founders of a strategic insights firm, TomorrowToday Global. We both have the privilege and opportunity to speak, present, consult, and facilitate on the changing world of work and leadership across multiple sectors and geographies. As we do so, we regard ourselves as 'ignorant maestros' – a wonderfully descriptive oxymoron borrowed from Israeli conductor Itay Talgam. In this book, we will share the new type of leadership required for the turbulent times in which we live, new approaches to developing these leaders, and new ways of thinking about leadership. We say 'new', but of course many of our thoughts, suggestions, and insights have origins in the work of others. We take to heart the words of Isaac Newton, who in 1675 said, 'If I have seen further it is by standing on the shoulders of Giants.'

The first section of the book looks at the changing context for leadership. We start in chapter 1 by providing a context for a style of leadership known as 'adaptive leadership'. Chapter 2 looks at the specific context of the 2020s and what we believe will be a remarkable decade of change. Chapter 3 then looks backwards, with an overview of key historical eras and the leadership competencies that were required for each of them – building to a picture of where we are today, and the

necessity for an adaptive approach. Chapter 4 outlines the need to adapt (or die) and what it takes to be adaptively intelligent.

Chapter 5 links leadership to the future and emphasizes the importance of new thinking and new mindsets for leadership. It introduces three key capabilities leaders need to develop in order to be adaptive, which are then unpacked in detail in the following three chapters: chapter 6 looks at curiosity and asking great questions, chapter 7 looks at the lost arts of feedback and reflection, and chapter 8 unpacks the issue of bias in our thinking.

In chapter 9, we introduce a model of leadership that makes sense of the adaptive world. It's called invitational leadership, and is a powerful framework for use in any leadership context. In some ways this is the heart of our book, presenting a deeply researched leadership model that emerges from and makes sense of the changing world around us.

Armed with this model of leadership, we then suggest five vital issues that leaders need to rethink: diversity, storytelling, technology, experimentation, and leadership development. Chapters 10 through 14 take each of these five issues in turn and invite leaders to rethink both the theory and practice of leadership for the 2020s.

Chapter 15 provides a note of caution, warning leaders of what could happen if we don't look after ourselves and allow the changing world to overwhelm us. Balance is essential for the adaptive leader.

Chapter 16 concludes the book with a call to action: to do and to be.

Before you start with the book proper, let us remind you that essentially 'you lead out of who you are'. This means that the leadership journey differs from person to person and is one that is as much 'inwards' as it is 'outwards'. Given this, we would encourage you to take your time in reading this book. Take it in small bites – one chapter at a time, reflecting on what you have read and thinking about what it means for your leadership practice. It might be helpful to journal as you make your way through these pages, and by the end, the real value might be what you have 'discovered' through your reflection and journaling.

We hope that this book adds value to your leadership journey. We hope it provides the catalyst in your own learning, unlearning, and relearning as a leader. We hope it makes a tangible difference in both how you think about and how you practice the art of leadership in a changing world. We know it is no easy task leading in the complexity that is today's context and, like you, we regard ourselves as fellow learners on this magical journey of exploring leadership in a changing world.

Enjoy the read. Enjoy the journey.

In addition to the book, you can visit www.tomorrowtodayglobal.com/leading-in-a-changing-world-2021 for additional video resources from our team and community - helping leaders and their teams deal with the disruption that 2020 threw our way, and the disruption that will continue throughout the 2020s.

1. The Hazy Horizon: Leading When the Path Is Unclear

'The thinking that created the problems we are facing will not generate the solutions that we need.' Albert Einstein

It was a cold December in 1862. It wasn't just the weather; the mood of the young nation of America was also frosty. For nearly two years the Civil War had been raging and no end was yet in sight. As President Abraham Lincoln looked ahead to the coming year, he knew that in just a few weeks he would sign the Emancipation Proclamation to free America's slaves, thus cementing the divide between North and South that had started the war in the first place. Sensing the need to strengthen the resolve of the nation's leaders, he sent a written message to Congress outlining his plans and thoughts. The sentiments expressed are as true and apt for us today as they were back then, especially in this concluding paragraph:

> 'The dogmas of the quiet past are inadequate to the stormy present. The occasion is piled high with difficulty, and we must rise with the occasion. As our case is new, so we must think anew, and act anew. We must disenthrall ourselves, and then we shall save our country.'

The world in which we find ourselves today is no less fraught with challenge and change than Lincoln's was over 150 years ago. We face tremendous challenges to our way of life, from sources as diverse as new technologies, religious extremism, economic uncertainty, and significant social change, amongst others. Our world is changing, and the paths to the future are hazy. Just as in Lincoln's time, the difference between success and failure will come down to leadership and the choices that we all make.

So, *we* too need to think anew, act anew, and disenthrall *ourselves* from the dogmas of *our* past. Our world is changing – maybe more now than at any time in living memory.

We need to free ourselves up to accept the times in which we find ourselves, and make the kinds of decisions that will secure our future. We cannot merely rely on past experiences or established systems to do this. It's time to rewrite the rules – or maybe just accept that the rules are being rewritten and embrace the new world that is emerging around us.

This is going to require new approaches in every aspect of society. Not least, it's going to require new approaches to leadership and what it means to be a leader.

If the world is changing, then leadership needs to change too. And we know that the world is definitely changing!

All of which brings us to what it will take to lead in the 'new world of work'.

Leading in a 'new world of work'

Leadership always occurs within a context. If the world around us – including the global systems, our industry, our organisation, and our team – is changing dramatically, then our definitions of what good leadership looks like also need to change. The type of leadership required – the leader that will be most successful – is the one that best reflects the context within which it operates. But what is this context?

There are three fundamental forces causing deep structural change in our world right now: technology, institutions, and social values.

Technology has transformed the way in which we do business. Never before has so much information been available to so many, so quickly. In the past, information was powerful when only a few people had it, and so it was guarded and protected.

Today, exactly the opposite is true: information is valuable only as far as it is shared. Old mindsets towards information, especially the mistaken belief that one can 'manage information', are constantly being shown up for what they are: old, outdated, and in our current context, erroneous. The belief that we can 'manage information' is simply a modern-day business paradox.

Take, for example, the approach of IBM. In 2018, IBM registered 9,100 patents – the most of any company in the USA. It was the 26th year in a row that they had topped the patents registration list. Yet, back in 2005, they had announced that they would regularly release some of their patents, inviting people to use them. Tesla did something similar in early 2019, making all of their patents and designs open-source and saying that Tesla 'will not initiate patent lawsuits against anyone who, in good faith, wants to use our technology'. This follows a similar announcement made by Elon Musk when he unveiled SpaceX's plans to build a spaceship capable of reaching Mars in 2016: 'Compete with us, or collaborate with us, we don't mind. Let's just get this done.'

Leaders who fail to get to grips with the implications of this change driver are riding a horse that is already dead in the starting stall. When that bell sounds (and it sounded some time ago) they are left for dead. Technology has changed and will continue to change business models, and current leaders cannot afford to ignore or assume that they will not be affected by the ever-evolving nature of technology, with all its opportunities and threats.

When it comes to the *institutions* in which we work, it is apparent that the nature of the beast is changing. Central organisational models, supported by impressive hierarchical structures, chains of command, and clearly defined functions, are giving way to decentralised models. In these decentralised models, power and decision-making are being pushed to the boundaries, or as Jonas Ridderstrale and Kjell Nordstrom in *Karaoke Capitalism* (2004) refer to it, the 'brains are at the borders'.

The clearly delineated job descriptions and functions are giving way to multi-tasking, flexibility, and mobility. If hierarchical towers serve as a caricature of the modern corporation, the market square better denotes the emerging postmodern institution through which we now do business in the global context. In a world where nimble dexterity is an essential business characteristic, central hierarchies offer ponderous decision-making with the added disadvantage that those making the decisions are usually far removed from the battlefield. Old-style hierarchies reward longevity and experience, and are places where rank and authority are ingrained through title and privilege. The values and mechanisms used to keep this status quo well-oiled and functioning are a thing of the past – to all but those still astride this dead horse that is!

Altering the structures to reflect and take advantage of these changes occurring through technology and shifting values is easier written about than done. In the process, some strong corporate moulds have to be smashed and resistance overcome. It requires savvy leadership, appropriate timing, and determination if it is to succeed.

In some of the organisations in which TomorrowToday Global has been involved, we have seen just how difficult it is to make structural changes. Things that would seem easy to change (reserved parking, titles, offices – to name just a few) are met with howls of protest and deep-seated unhappiness by those who perceive themselves to be the victims in the process. These are the very things that when discussed with no threat of actual change are met with, 'it's not that important'. In reality, they prove to be anything but unimportant when change actually occurs (in much the same way that the prefacing words 'with all due respect' usually signal the launch of an all-out attack, and should really be taken to mean 'with no real respect').

Listen out for those words in your next meeting!

Consider also shifting *social values*. Leadership is being impacted by the change that can be seen in who it is that walks through the front doors of your business every day.

These people not only are your staff, but also form part of your customer, client, and supplier base and generally populate the people chain of which you are part. We are talking about the generation referred to interchangeably as Generation Y and Millennials. They are a vast generation that looks and acts unlike the Baby Boomers and Gen Xers who preceded them, and understanding their values becomes key to interpreting their behaviour. The point is that Generation Y behaviour, driven by their underpinning values, stands in stark contrast to that of those with whom they share their workspace. The contrasting work behaviour between these generations is causing mayhem in most companies as bosses find themselves at a loss as to how best to attract, retain, motivate, and reward the 'Bright Young Things' – the talent that they know they need to retain if they are to sustain and extend their success.

Leadership which fails to understand the fundamental differences in values that is driving such behaviour is liable to employ the wrong methodologies in attempting to lead Generation Y. A simple example of this difference is the contrasting way in how the different generations approach authority and respect.

Boomers (born in the 1950s and 60s) see authority as structural – they respect those with titles, positions, and those who are above them in the hierarchy. For Generation X (born 1970s and 80s), respect has to be earned and has nothing to do with title or position. Gen Y (defined differently by different authors, but normally considered to be born between 1984 – 2000) understand authority structures, but see themselves as valuable contributors and will question authority at every turn. They only respect authority that is used for the good of others. We are now beginning to see Gen Z (born 2000 – 2020) enter the workplace, and our experience of them in the education system shows a different engagement again with authority – one that understands and appreciates authority, but is prepared to challenge it on the basis of principles and shifting values. Failure to understand these generational differences can lead to both wrong approaches and assumptions being made.

*For more detailed information on generations, see the book Graeme Codrington co-authored with Sue Grant-Marshall, **Mind the Gap**.*

The new generations are looking for different things when joining a company. They need change, flexibility, informality, and information. They are individualistic (bad news for the traditional team-building initiatives) and are asking different questions of their employers.

Once we were told by the person who heads up talent development at Johnson & Johnson that he had been asked by one of their 'Bright Young Things' whether or not it was okay to bring his dog to work! The questions being asked are changing, and underpinning the questions are different expectations and values.

Making sense of sense-making

It is not difficult for leaders to stay in touch with the changes that are occurring in all these fields of technology, institutions, and values (people); the difficult part is acting on it. Many attempts at harnessing the opportunities these change drivers deliver result in cosmetic responses rather than the deep-seated changes that are required.

At a recent Business Leaders Workshop, our team asked the 60 or so participants what their biggest organisational needs were right now. Nearly one third rated 'understanding changing business contexts' as their most important business need, and nearly half rated this as very important to them right now. In our work with companies around the world, across every industry and sector, we've seen this same issue over and over again.

It is indicative of business leaders who are more comfortable operating in conditions of certainty now finding themselves in a sustained era of uncertainty and change.

Recent reports from Deloitte UK indicate that public companies are stockpiling cash at historically high levels – in the UK alone, public companies had over £60 billion in cash in their reserves in early 2015. The main reason for this is that these companies just don't know what to do. Holding cash does not generate jobs, does not grow profits, and has been proven to ensure the company will underperform in the market; in other words, it is not clever. But business leaders would rather do nothing than do the wrong thing. For all their talk of innovation, when the chips are down, they'd prefer caution and inactivity. They just don't know what to do right now.

Not that they would admit this, of course. And there's lots of 'busy-ness' inside their businesses. But their strategic actions speak loudly.

As we write this update in early 2019, in many parts of the world companies continue to hold on to their cash. In 2018, for example, President Trump in America oversaw a massive corporate tax break for companies, claiming that it would kickstart the economy. Instead, the company owners used the money to pay themselves dividends, or kept the money locked up in their companies. They'd prefer cautious conservatism to optimistic investment in the future.

Deep structural, disruptive change is the norm in the world at the moment. We are living through more than an era of change. We have reached an inflection point in history and are now living in an era where processes, systems, structures, products, services, and careers no longer change – they transform.

The bad news

The bad news is that this era is not going to go away. We firmly believe that the overwhelming majority of change we're going to experience in our lifetimes is still ahead of us. By the end of this decade, technology will transform how we sell, market, communicate, interact, collaborate, innovate, lead, train, and educate. The transformation that is underway will have an impact on every business process and every person we connect with. Successful companies will therefore be those capable of transformation, and not just change. And that's going to require a lot of understanding about changing business contexts.

The worse news

In a disruptive world, having a disruptive innovation capability is essential – not just for growing new markets, but also for protecting your existing ones. But leading disruptive innovation requires new mindsets, attitudes, and behaviours from your leaders – and within your organisation itself. Books like Clayton Christensen's *The Innovator's*

Dilemma (2016 updated edition), authors and speakers like Seth Godin, the remarkable success of innovators like Apple and Google, and the high-profile failures of Blockbuster, HMV, Borders, and Kodak have heightened the awareness of, and fuelled a desire for, game-changing innovation. More resources, models, and tools exist to help companies innovate than ever before. And yet, most public companies are doing nothing. They're sitting on their cash. They're unable to make sense of the complexity of the changing business environment around them.

Many business leaders have risen through the ranks of management where predictability and control are valued and rewarded. But now disruptive times generate levels of constant uncertainty very unlike this. Unexpected events, constant change, new information, inevitable failures, and a fundamental lack of control are inherent to the new world of work. Few leaders are formally prepared to deal with the realities of leading or responding to this type of disruption – especially when it is incessant.

We don't have to look far for examples of the effects of sustained disruptive change: the music, entertainment, pharmaceutical, computing, communications, travel, estate agency (in fact, any agencies), book publishing, photography, and healthcare industries have all experienced dramatic change due to new technologies, business models, distribution channels, lead times, pricing models, regulations, and market expectations. Companies in these industries have had no option but to experiment and introduce new technologies, methodologies, and business models – not just to compete but to survive.

Many have not survived. And generally, this can be attributed to a failure of leadership, and a failure of the leaders to make good, assured, timeous strategic decisions.

The challenge for organisations of all types is that the competencies necessary for leading through disruptive change are not formulaic or quantifiable. There are no 1-2-3 easy steps to follow to ensure success. And even models and methods that work today might not work again tomorrow. As Gary Hamel says in *The Future of Management* (2007): 'New problems demand new principles. Put bluntly, there's simply no way to build tomorrow's essential organisational capabilities – resilience, innovation, and employee engagement – atop the scaffolding of 20th-century management principles... In an age of wrenching change and hyper-competition, the most valuable human capabilities are precisely those that are least manageable.'

The good news

The primary focus of leaders in volatile, disruptive times should be to make sense of the times for their team. The good news is that most good leaders should be able to shift easily into this success-building mindset. But the key is simply that: a change in mindset.

This mindset shift involves at least the following:

- Recognising that we live in an era of remarkable change and disruption that is not going to go away for at least another decade.
- Doing nothing is not an option.
- Don't look for one-size-fits-all solutions.
- Understanding that best principles are much better than best practices (in fact, best practices can be downright dangerous).
- You need to unlearn and relearn – not just once, but over and over again. Question your assumptions.
- Knowing that what got you here won't get you there. New leadership competencies are required. (This might mean you're not as good as you think you are as a leader.)

- Embracing paradox. Think right-right instead of right-wrong. Learn new ways of thinking that rely on looking for new patterns and connections.
- Pushing your own personal boundaries. Every day.
- Recognising that you will never have enough information ever again. You can't let this stop you from deciding, and acting.
- Realising that you don't need to be able to see the whole path in order to take the first step. (This is a huge lesson that corporate managers can learn from serial entrepreneurs.)
- Not preventing uncertainty. Stop avoiding surprises.
- Embracing diversity and encouraging differences of opinion.
- Going on the offensive: create disruption, don't just wait for it.
- Taking time to make sense of a changing world. As a leader this is your primary task: sense-making.
- Communicating more. Listening more.

This is not a random list. Please read it again and honestly assess yourself: How many of these concepts are you already applying? In this book, you'll find lots of examples and practical tips on how to go about this. But for now, ask yourself a simple question: Do you enjoy disruptive change, or do you attempt to avoid it?

Understanding our changing business context is something we can learn to do. We can develop horizon-scanning techniques. We can build new approaches to flexible strategies and use scenario-based planning. We can work on personal adaptability, creativity, and resilience. We can improve our thinking and analytical skills. We can implement any number of change processes in our businesses, and change what we measure and reward to support these. We can – and must – do all of these things, and more, if we're to be successful.

But first – and most importantly – we must change our mindset about the era we're in and what it means to be living in a time of constant, disruptive change. It really is as simple – and as tough – as that.

2. Inflection Points and Building Blocks for the Future

'There will be more change in the next 15 years than there has been in the last 50 years.' Bill Gates (2015)

In 1900, New York City had a problem. Actually, it probably had many problems, but one of the main ones was how to clear the streets of horse manure. At the start of the previous century, over 100,000 horses produced over 2.5 million pounds (over 1.13 million kilograms) of manure *every day* just in the city limits of New York. There was genuine concern that the streets of major cities around the world could literally be buried under metres of manure. In 1900, an international urban planning conference was scheduled for 10 days in New York. It was abandoned after three days as no one could foresee any solution to the problem.

Yet, just over a decade later, pictures from 1912 and later show an entirely transformed New York City. The age of the automobile arrived fast and furious (even if the cars weren't able to drift!). Pictures from that decade show mainly Ford Model Ts dominating city transportation, with not a horse in sight. And all in under ten years.

A more recent example of the same breathtaking rate of change, when systems change, comes from the cover of the 12 November 2007 *Forbes* magazine. The headline states: 'Nokia: One billion customers; can anyone catch the cellphone king?' Just a few months earlier, on 29 June 2007, Steve Jobs had unveiled Apple's iPhone. Many industry experts had scoffed at a computer company making phones. History, of course, tells a different story. Within a decade, Nokia had all but disappeared, and been sold to Microsoft, whilst Apple had become the world's most valuable company.

Both of these examples show us that when the system changes, it changes quickly. Both these examples are reminders that the system can change – the current market players do not have to remain that way forever. And now, of course, we could add all the examples you've already grown very bored of hearing at every conference you've been to in the last five years: Uber, Airbnb, Netflix, and Tesla are talked about so much at the moment that we're in danger of ignoring how truly disruptive they actually are.

But we must not ignore them.

The nature of exponential change is that for a very long time it appears as if nothing is happening: nothing happens; nothing happens; nothing happens; and then suddenly everything happens. When all the moving parts align, suddenly the machine hums into life. For motor vehicles and cities, it was the confluence of advances in steel manufacturing, improvements in the internal combustion engine design, the continuous production line of Ford Motor Company, and changes in society that resulted in a system change. These systemic changes were accelerated by some key decisions made and implemented by leaders at the time.

Reflecting on this era, Shoshana Zuboff, in *The Age of Surveillance Capitalism* (2019), states: 'Everything would have to be reinvented: new technologies, yes, but these would have to reflect new ways of fulfilling people's needs; a new economic model that could turn those new practices into profit; and a new social contract that could sustain it all. The citizens, consumers, executives, workers, lawmakers, jurists, scholars, journalists, managers, and public officials who undertook this effort stepped into unknown territory.'

Henry Ford was part of stepping into the unknown. Ford understood that farmers, shopkeepers, ordinary people, and especially the people who worked in his factories wanted to own cars too. But they couldn't afford them. In one (possibly apocryphal) weekend, Ford calculated that people needed to earn $5 a day in order to afford the cars his factories were building. He asked his team how much they were earning, and it was half that, so he ordered that their wages be doubled. Just like that. He was right – they started buying his cars. Everyone did.

And the system changed.

For smartphones, the system change happened with the confluence of increasing power and simultaneous drop in price of computer chips, the increased capacity and drop in price of digital storage, and the improvement in battery technology – all these things, along with the vision of Steve Jobs, made the iPhone possible. Any company could have created a smartphone; Apple just got there first.

And then some interesting competitors joined them. In 2007, you might have bought a fridge or TV from Samsung, but not a phone. You might have Googled the answer to a question on your computer's browser, but you wouldn't have thought to use their software to power your phone.

How quickly things can change. When last did you even see a Nokia phone, let alone use one? The system changed, and Nokia was left behind.

The message of these examples should be clear: beware of sudden system changes.

Our message to you is equally clear: we are living in an era that will make those earlier times of disruption look like child's play. In almost every industry, there are new rules for success and failure. Long-established norms are being shattered, and new competitors are 'playing the game' in very different ways.

These moments of deep structural change are called inflection points, and we're about to experience the most significant one in recorded history.

Is it really changing THAT much?

It is not unreasonable to ask whether the era we live in *really* is as remarkable as all that. Do we *really* live in an unprecedented time in history, and even if we do, does leadership (and followership) *really* need to change? It's not unreasonable to ask these questions. But it is clear that the answer is unequivocal: we definitely are living in unprecedented times of deep structural change.

If you cannot see the evidence in your industry yet, you won't have long to wait. Alec Ross, in *The Industries of the Future* (2015), puts it this way: 'In business areas as far afield as life sciences, finance, warfare, and agriculture, if you can imagine an advance, somebody is already working on how to develop and commercialize it.'

But, as we have seen, it is less about these individual advances, and more about the confluence of systems.

When the systems change

We have spent the past few decades creating the building blocks for deep structural change.

The hype at management conferences for the past decade (from the World Economic Forum at Davos to the regional accounting officers forum in your part of the world) has been around a number of emerging technologies that have been variously labelled 'The Fourth Industrial Revolution'. (Though most people who use the label can't describe the first three revolutions in any detail, let alone the defining features of the fourth!)

There is a danger in getting caught up in the hype of the emerging technologies that are driving change in the world, and missing two important issues: (1) the more important issue is the change in systems, and (2) business models are much more important than business cases (or, put another way, changes in technologies are a lot less significant than changes in business models).

Over and over again, business leaders fail to recognise where they are on Gartner's Hype Cycle curve, and fail to recognise that the 'Trough of Disillusionment' comes just before the real money starts to be made. That's what led Nokia to believe that iPhones were 'just a fad' (an actual quote from Nokia's marketing director in January 2008). It is what caused people to ignore the shift to alternative energy sources until just a few years ago, even though it was clear that the price of photovoltaics was dropping precipitously. It is what is causing people to discount the coming driverless car revolution – waiting until they are 100% safe before even considering adopting them. Or plastic manufacturers to not realise their entire industry is nearly at an end. This list could go on and on. It is amazing how easy some people find it to chase shiny new technologies without actually seeing the systemic changes that they will cause.

This is why one of the most important leadership tasks is to provide context. And it is why leadership itself has to change.

If we're living in a new world, then new approaches to leadership are required. But are we *really* living in such a new world? Isn't this just a blip in history that will soon be over? Isn't history always changing anyway? It's easy to think that maybe all we need to do to survive this crazy moment we live in right now is just grit our teeth a little bit longer and wait for sanity to return, and then our existing models will still be valid. Hopefully soon, we think, the current madness will subside and then we can get back to 'business as usual'.

But this is not going to happen. The signs are everywhere and they're all pointing in one direction: we are living through one of those moments in history when all the rules for success and failure get rewritten. We're living through a period of structural change and realignment. Every so often, history stops its relentless forward march, takes an abrupt turn, and heads off in a new direction. This is often linked to a new technological development, which changes how people live, interact, and work. We name these moments in history to mark their importance: the Industrial Revolution, the Reformation, the Enlightenment, the Renaissance, and changes in dynasties.

Think, for example, of what the world was like before the Industrial Revolution – and then after. Before and after electricity, indoor plumbing, engines, trains and cars, telegraphs and telephones, and machines. These innovations all flooded into the world during a remarkable period in the latter half of the 19th century, and the world was changed forever.

We are living through one of those eras now. The rules for success and failure in society, industries, and every organisation everywhere are being rewritten. It can be frightening and disconcerting for individuals and organisations alike. Disruptive change like this brings many threats as well as significant opportunities – but only for the brave, the bold, and those willing to adjust their mindsets to a new world. And only for those who recognise the era for what it is.

3. New Rules for a New Era

'Every few hundred years in Western history there occurs a sharp transformation... Fifty years later, there is a new world. And the people born then cannot even imagine the world in which their grandparents lived.' Peter Drucker

As we saw in the previous chapter, the most significant shifts in history are those that cause structural change to the institutions and systems of society. When this happens, new winners and losers emerge, and the nature of competition changes.

Competitive advantage has always existed, and understanding the evolution of what constitutes competitive advantage in today's context is important for any business. It may seem obvious, and yet there are many companies that persist in playing by 'old rules' when it comes to how they endeavour to create a competitive advantage for their service or product. A way to understand today's competitive advantage – and for many it will strategically be 'tomorrow's competitive advantage' – is to 'go back to the future'.

By tracing what constituted competitive advantage through a succession of economic eras, we are able to see the evolution of what remains central to business success. This journey through time builds an appreciation for how each new era precipitates what we could call the 'rules of the game' in the quest to establish a competitive advantage. The secret is in understanding these changes to the rules of the game and, of course, interpreting them into one's own context and practice. This is not always easy. The inability to do this is a contributing factor in the fall from grace that has beset many companies, which at one or another time might have appeared impregnable as they strode like a colossus across their particular industry.

What follows then in this chapter is a sprint through 10,000 years of human history viewed through a lens of economic eras, in which we pick out what constituted competitive advantage in each of the eras examined. Naturally this represents a highly summarised overview; nonetheless, there are valuable insights to be gained for future success through undertaking such a journey.

The Hunter-Gatherer Economy

In the first era of recorded human history, life was nomadic and tribal. Past experience was essential to both survival and the transfer of knowledge. It stands to reason then that the elders were the leaders within the tribe. Those whose stories stretched back the furthest were the leaders. Remembering was revered as it was essential to survival. In this era, achieving a greater sense of focus than your competitors forged competitive advantage. By 'focus' it is meant the ability to hunt or to gather food, ensure the tribe's safety, and act on vital knowledge. In essence, the ability to take action or translate this 'sense of focus' secured a competitive advantage. In this economy, leadership would have devolved to the strongest of the species. In the tribal context, this meant that men would have exerted dominance when it came to leadership matters.

Summary of the Hunter-Gatherer Economy

- Competitive advantage: Focus
- Leadership: The strong
- Time: Historical
- Disruptive shift: The plough, harnessing animal power

The disruptive shift that occurred, which changed the rules of the game, was the ability to harness animal power to plough – and of course the plough itself. One way to understand 'disruptive shift' is to tag it 'technology'. This is a consistent lever in the transition from one era (economy) to the next. Technology is always the 'game changer' and is also a simplistic way to understand the respective transitions that we are exploring. In reality, it is not this simple. We know that events – local and global, as well as other factors – also have an impact on such transitions. However, for our purposes, we will concentrate purely on the major technologies that served as a catalyst to the rules of the game changing when it came to competitive advantage.

The Agrarian Economy

The plough, the advent of animal husbandry, and the invention of the water mill all led to an increase in available energy. In essence, muscle power was replaced by this ability to harness animal power and nature. The nomadic nature of tribal life gave way to permanent homesteads that combined both life and work. All contributed, and having children guaranteed a succession plan was in place.

In this context, competitive advantage was forged by those who were able to extract more from their main asset – their land – than others. Those who understood the benefits of subsistence farming and were able to practice it created for themselves a competitive advantage. 'Sweating your assets', it would seem, is a phrase that is rooted deeply in the past as this is exactly what it took to create a competitive advantage in the Agrarian Economy. Leadership in this context centred on those who owned the land.

Summary of the Agrarian Economy

- Competitive advantage: Working your main asset

- Leadership: The landowners
- Time: Cyclical
- Disruptive shift: The steam engine, the printing press

The disruptive shift that occurred was the beginning of the Industrial Revolution, which started in Britain around 1750.

The Industrial Economy

Innovations such as the printing press and the steam engine were to revolutionise society and lead to rapid urbanisation and a redistribution of the population mass. Factories emerged and, with this, work became organised. This was the birth of modern-day management as Fredrick Taylor and others proposed theories around how best to maximise efficiencies in the pursuit of profitability. It is in this era that organisational hierarchies emerged and the logic that produced clichés such as 'if you can't measure it, you can't manage it' and 'if it isn't broken, don't fix it'. A clear distinction between the bosses (management) and the workers emerged – or between the 'white collar' and 'blue collar' workers as they became known. Management provided the 'head' (the eyes, ears, and brain) power and the workers the 'body' (the muscle) power.

The Industrial Era has cast a long shadow, one that still has many a contemporary company in its shade. Our current management systems (which can be traced back to the Industrial Era) are designed to bring about compliance – and they are successful. Achieving greater business efficiencies forged competitive advantage in the Industrial Economy. The irrepressible force to achieve such efficiencies is evidenced in the production line assembly system made famous by Henry Ford.

In the Industrial Economy, leadership was transferred to those who were the factory owners – the educated. Access to education was limited and, in some cases, restricted – and those who were able to exploit the benefits of access to education became the leaders. The uneven distribution of global wealth accelerated and the dichotomy between wealth and poverty within society became ever more pronounced. Time shifted from the cyclical (in the Agrarian Economy) to the linear as a bright future beckoned through the never-ending wave of technological advances.

The disruptive shift that occurred happened in the 1960s with the arrival of technologies that elevated our ability to access and store information.

Summary of the Industrial Economy:

- Competitive advantage: Business efficiencies
- Leadership: The educated
- Time: Linear
- Disruptive shift: Information technologies

The Information Economy

The early mark of the fourth economy was the emergence and/or dominance of companies such as Hewlett-Packard, IBM, and Motorola. Knowledge overtook capital in importance as capital shifted from being physical to intellectual, or as Rolf Jensen phrases it in *The Dream Society* (1999), '[capital] resides in our heads, not in bank accounts or in machines'.

In the same way that the Industrial Economy 'abolished' manual labour by replacing it with machines, so the Information Economy has taken over much of the cerebral and sensory work done by humans. This has happened through the increasing use of computers and intelligent machines to perform those functions once done by people. The Information Economy has grown exponentially with the rapid and pervasive technological innovations that have occurred. Omnipresent telecommunications, 24/7 TV channels, personal computers, and smartphones are the obvious examples.

In this economy, competitive advantage could no longer be found in ensuring greater business efficiencies. As with all the other economies, when the transition occurs, the old factors that secured a competitive advantage become merely an entry-level requirement. In the Information Economy, competitive advantage is found in the ability to extract relevant information from within and without the system – and use that information to create a strategic advantage. It's called 'business intelligence'.

In this economy, companies mine data or pay others to do so on their behalf. This part of the equation is understood – the need to have access to data. However, having the data is not enough; one has to show it and use it in ways that people both understand and find helpful. In a world where business efficiency reigned supreme, many large multinationals created silos within their structures. These silos are often limited in their ability to communicate with each other. Now that the world has shifted to a more integrated context, this inability to share relevant information rapidly leads to a distinct disadvantage – especially when the customers' or consumers' expectations are for speedy, integrated service or delivery. For a current example of this, think no further than many of the large banks.

In the Information Economy, time moves from linear to being open-ended. It becomes 'real time'. Reality is portrayed live and events, even though separated by distance, become simultaneously experienced in a world that is increasingly connected. Leadership is centred on those who have access to the data and who display agility and nimbleness in the face of the insistent, rapid, and ubiquitous change that has become the new norm. Leadership previously was very often given to the most qualified and 'professional' members of the team, with lawyers, engineers, and accountants leading the pack in the corporate world.

An interesting footnote in tracing leadership throughout the respective economies is that the Information Age is the first economic era conducive to women assuming leadership roles. This is not to say that there were no women leaders in the other eras, but simply that the context did not support women in leadership positions and roles. For example, in the Hunter-Gatherer Era, leadership would devolve to the physically strongest – men were stronger; in the Agrarian Economy, it would have been the landowners – women were generally forbidden to own land or have the title deeds; in the Industrial Economy, leadership fell to the educated – women were prohibited from accessing tertiary educational institutes. In the Information Economy, for the first time, women were not obviously prejudiced in their aspirations to formally occupy leadership roles and positions. It is little surprise then that in the corporate world, it was the information technology sector that led the way in appointing female CEOs.

Summary of the Information Economy

- Competitive advantage: The ability to extract and use information
- Leadership: Those with access to information technologies, and the professions that are based on deep, industry-specific knowledge
- Time: Open-ended, reality
- Disruptive shift: Social technologies and ubiquitous access to information

The disruptive shift now occurring is the rapid advance of social technologies, which are changing the rules of the game in how we connect, collaborate, and communicate, combined with ubiquitous access to information that destroys some of the mystique around the professions. Consider, for example, how we've shifted from trusting our family doctor's every word to now double-checking what he or she says on NetDoctor.com.

The Connection Economy

The Information Economy is giving way to the next era: the 'Connection Economy'. The new economic era has also been referred to as the 'Relationship Economy', the 'Experience Economy', and even Rolf Jensen's 'Dream Society'. It really does not matter what descriptive title you ascribe to it – the point is that once again the rules of the game are shifting and, with that, what constitutes competitive advantage.

It is a shift that is an extension of the use of technology, not merely to extract business data but also to use it for personal connection. It is the emergence of social platforms (Facebook, LinkedIn, Twitter, etc.) and a social mindset (think of TripAdvisor, Uber, Airbnb, Kickstarter, and others) that connect people and are used to initiate, develop, and establish personal relationships. It is an era in which the value of stored or protected information is diminishing, and the value of shared information increasing.

The Connection Economy is being played out against the backdrop of a 'changing of the guard' within both the work force and leadership domains inside organisations. Essentially it is a clash between Boomers (who could at best be described as 'digital immigrants') and Gen Y /Millennials and Gen Z ('digital natives'), and it is on the battleground of this generational 'war' where it is easiest to see the emergence of the

Connection Economy. The clash in values between Boomers and Gen Y/Z, when it comes to work-life balance, work ethic, career development, change, teamwork, and motivators (to name but a few), is pronounced.

Technology – and specifically the use of social technologies – forms the cutting edge to this generational divide.

In the Connection Economy, competitive advantage shifts to the ability to form meaningful connections or relationships, and one's willingness to share information with others. In the context of access to information, personal choice, and competitive pricing, the question of 'why buy your product or engage your service?' becomes ever narrower. The decision comes down to personal 'connection': I want to do business with you because I like you, trust you, I believe in your cause, your values – we have a relationship, and because I am impressed by what other people (even strangers) have to say about you.

Perhaps the most obvious arena in which to see and understand this shift is in what has been dubbed the 'war for talent'. The attraction and retention of 'talent' (the next generation) is paramount to any organisation's future. Talent has become big business, and for all the activity and effort in this area, few are getting it right. Essentially, it is a connection issue. Attracting, retaining, and engaging talent is all about connecting with a group who, for the most part, looks, thinks, and acts differently from those who have gone before. Those responsible for writing the existing 'rules of business' are under such siege.

The Connection Economy sees a shift towards meaningful relationships both inside and outside your organisation. Public relations has to be turned inwards. Social technology and a generation who knows how to use it (in fact, who cannot imagine life without it) are driving a different agenda around the why, how, and what when it comes to connecting. In an economy where connection is essential, many IT policies appear archaic and require serious rethinking (more of this in chapter 12).

Leadership in the Connection Economy will pass to those who understand the fundamental shift taking place and what that means for their own leadership thinking and practices. The term 'authentic leadership' is making its appearance with ever-increasing frequency in leadership development programmes; emotional intelligence is gaining ground, and the host of tools associated with how to measure and develop it (a trap of Industrial Age thinking perhaps?). There is a growing appreciation for understanding leadership as a 'character ethic' rather than merely a 'skillset'. There is greater urgency in ensuring that 'who we say we are' as a company is 'who we really are'. It is an alignment between the corporate values and the corporate behaviour. It is a consistency being driven by a connected generation arriving at work unafraid to ask questions in this area – and unafraid to share their findings with their extensive networks.

Further evidence of the emergence of the Connection Economy is the increasing emphasis being given to 'social business' – a term that would have been something of an oxymoron to an earlier generation! Welcome to the Connection Economy! It is a context in which time is virtual, and one which is forcing a serious rethink in areas such as organisational design and structure, strategy, leadership, marketing, public relations, and training and development.

Summary of the Connection Economy

- Competitive advantage: Authentic connection – inside and outside your business, and a willingness to share and collaborate
- Leadership: The emotionally intelligent and connected

- Time: Virtual
- Disruptive shift: (?) A good question to be asking... watch this space and keep looking out the window!

Making a successful transition

As business and society have transitioned between each economic era, the competitive advantages of the past era have become a mere entry criteria – still important to the proper functioning, but no longer a source of sustainable advantage. For example: Focus, assets, business efficiency, and data – the competitive advantages of previous economic eras – are still important for success in the Connection Economy, but today these are increasingly only minimum requirements for competitiveness. To succeed in the Connection Economy, business leaders are required to up their game and create authentic relationships with the 'tribes' who choose to engage with their business. The key words today are Choice, Connection, Permission, and Relationships. The bar has once again been raised, adding further complexity to business success. Those leaders who recognise this shift and act first will gain competitive advantage in the Connection Economy.

The ability to transition from one economic era to the next is fundamental to continued and sustained business success. Few manage to achieve this in a world of increasing complexity and ubiquitous and unrelenting change. However, smart leaders see the transition taking place and understand the need to build adaptability and nimbleness into the very DNA of their organisation.

4. Adapt or Die

'The illiterate of the 21ˢᵗ century will not be those who cannot read and write, but will be those who cannot learn, unlearn, and relearn.' Alvin Toffler, Future Shock (first published 1970)

Whilst we have spent a few chapters trying to lay out the context for the extraordinary change we believe we should expect in the future, Mark Mullen, CEO of Atom, is absolutely correct when he said, 'The future is uncertain. It is more important that you engineer agility and flexibility into your business than it is for you to know the future.'

From evolutionary biology we learn that survival is contingent on one's ability to adapt to changing circumstances. It is not necessarily the fittest, the strongest, the sexiest, or those with the biggest market share that survive (as we are often led to believe), but rather those most adaptable. This is an important distinction.

If we are living through an era of disruptive change, then *adaptability* will be a key skill for each of us to exhibit. How much more then will this be true for those tasked with leadership responsibilities! We call this set of skills 'adaptive intelligence'. The adaptability that is required will be both personal and organisational; it will require that we change both our leadership models as well as our business models.

Such times invite leaders to be learners and, through the very essence of what it means to be a learner, to adapt to the challenges at hand. Whilst this becomes essentially a personal challenge, the role of the leader means that they have to pursue this tough curriculum in the full glare of the public spotlight – of those both within and outside the organisation they lead. The nature of the leadership task means that they become accountable not only for the mindset, activity, and action of adapting themselves, but also for the very translation of such amongst those they lead.

The leader needs to recognise the nature of the challenge at hand: it is an 'adaptive challenge', which means that it is unlike anything that has previously been experienced (more on this in a moment). Leaders are leading their organisations and people into uncharted territory.

Consequently, a dependence on what worked in the past, coupled with the assumption of 'we have been here before', will prove fatal.

Yet for the most part, the old, outmoded, and well-worn perceptions surrounding leadership stubbornly refuse to go away. We often meet with senior leaders who express the desire to be more 'in control' – to assert their authority in a more convincing fashion in order to ensure their staff do exactly as they say. It often has to do with 'delivery' – and of course these leaders are right: it is about delivery. It is just that the way to go about it needs to change. The old 'command-and-control' mentality of leaders is, in today's world, as effective as attempting to harpoon a whale with a snorkel. And just as politically incorrect!

The confusion that leaders experience amidst the cacophony of 'experts' who hustle the latest trend or fad is just *how* to lead in an ever-changing world. In a global village where cultures collide and paradox is the norm, leadership is no easy task. Part of the problem is that there is an over-emphasis on the 'what' and 'how' of leadership at the expense of fostering a deeper understanding of the changing environment in which leadership takes place.

By neglecting the context for leadership, the result is that the practice has become dislocated from the underpinning theory. It is a serious situation. For one thing, it means that we unwittingly employ old practices in the face of new problems – with disastrous results. Invariably all that is accomplished is that we end up digging the hole that we are in deeper and faster! The emphasis on the *what* and the *how* has bred a market for the consumption of quick fixes, 'irrefutable laws', and tips booklets that have invaded the realm of leadership at the expense of genuine inquiry, authentic discussion, and bold experimentation. As a result, so much of leadership has become one-dimensional, stale, unimaginative, borrowed, and worst of all, irrelevant. It should be noted that those invested in the design and delivery of teaching leadership (leadership development programmes) carry much of the responsibility for this leadership wasteland.

What is it then that leaders need to pay attention to in the face of such an accusation?

There are two fundamental areas that any effective leader needs to explore, examine, and understand. Both these areas require constant work. In a nutshell, the two areas are: *themselves* and their *context*. Smart leaders know this and intentionally and instinctively work towards acquiring an ever-deepening understanding of both. It is the kind of work that requires both head and heart.

Smart leaders work hard at understanding themselves, which means exploring their own beliefs, principles, prejudices, and motivations. Interior landscaping is no longer optional for today's leaders and requires as much, if not more, sweat than that needed in mastering the many external skills that leadership demands. It has been on these external characteristics that leaders have long been judged – but that is about to change.

Adaptive leadership

One of the experts doing significant work on trying to understand what leadership should look like in these turbulent times is Prof Ronald Heifetz of Harvard. He has suggested a model he calls 'adaptive leadership'.

To explain the concept, he contrasts his model with traditional leadership (the type most iconically taught in MBA courses around the world). The traditional model might be called 'authoritative expertise'.

Authoritative expertise: In a world where the problems are known and the solutions clear, what we need is a leader who can 'get the job done'. This leader can deliver the desired results, using an agreed set of methods to deal with a clearly defined issue. We want these types of leaders when there is a crisis: the airplane's engine is on fire, a child is stuck in a tall tree, war breaks out, or when something life-threatening like open heart surgery or an armed bank robbery is taking place. Authoritative experts have been trained for these situations and have valuable experience.

We also value authoritative expertise during times of 'business as usual'. These leaders know what they're doing, they have experience, and we should do what they tell us to. When we *wish* for stability we long for this approach. It is therefore hardly surprising that against a global backdrop of uncertainty and volatility, political leadership in many parts of the world has swung to the right and to a more authoritarian form of national leadership.

As a team, we are often privileged to be asked to sit through senior leadership meetings with our clients. Right up to board level, these peepholes into our clients' workings provide valuable insights into not only their operations, but also (and most importantly) the culture of these organisations too. One abiding feature that concerns us greatly is how operational and tactical senior leadership meetings can become. This is baffling to us, but we think it relates to the comfort zone most senior leaders find in technical issues and authoritative expertise.

Ask yourself: In the last three leadership meetings you have attended, what proportion of the time in the meeting has been spent on tactical and operational issues, including micromanaging, firefighting, and reporting on details? Contrast this to how much time was spent on strategic issues, future trends, and systems-thinking?

Heifetz refers to past solutions as 'technical solutions', and he maintains that in the face of 'adaptive challenges', technical solutions simply will not work. What about those situations where the solutions are unclear, or even unknown? Even more difficult: What about those situations where the problem (or set of problems) is not clear? In these environments, authoritative experts can actually do untold damage. In these environments, we need adaptive leaders. Today, the environments requiring an adaptive approach are ever more common.

Adaptive challenges: By contrast, an adaptive challenge is one where past expertise is of little help, new patterns and systems are emerging, and therefore new approaches will be required. They have four key characteristics:

- The hearts and minds of people need to change, and choices must be made between contradictory values. Paradoxes are common when dealing with adaptive situations, with no clear 'right' answers.
- Technical fixes are not sufficient.
- Conflict persists, and it is often very difficult to see a compromise solution.

- If unaddressed, the situation will ultimately lead to crisis in the system or organisation.

You might be facing adaptive challenges when you find yourself saying to your team, 'Haven't we discussed this before?' Or, 'Didn't we speak about this last month?' Or, 'Why are we still talking about this issue? Why is it not yet resolved?' You might be facing an adaptive challenge when you keep coming up against the same issues, or having the same fights, or failing over and over to resolve behavioural or attitude problems in your team. The repetitive nature of problematic conversations, behaviours, and processes is a sure indication that you are meeting an adaptive challenge with technical solutions.

What you have been doing hasn't worked; it won't work; it will never work!

Adaptive challenges can be very difficult to deal with, and require a different type of leader and a different approach to leadership.

Adaptive leaders approach the world in different ways than the authoritative experts.

Adaptive leaders don't seek certainty when all around them the world is changing. Rather than wasting energy trying to stabilise what cannot be stabilised, adaptive leaders discover how best to balance when everything around them is shifting. They accept that past experiences won't help them and that they need to develop new skills and approaches for what confronts them now.

A few years ago, there was dramatic footage of a Pacific Sun cruise liner off the coast of New Zealand caught in very turbulent seas. The footage showed both people and furniture being swept from side to side as the ship rolled in the rough sea. Eventually one person was able to cling onto a pillar and thereby gain a semblance of stability whilst everything around them, including a grand piano, chairs, and tables, were hurtling from one end of the room to the other. The image of that one lone person, supporting himself with the pillar, forms a powerful image of 'stability in the midst of turbulence' that adaptive leadership demands. Trying to calm the sea was beyond the control of anyone; finding stability in the prevailing reality of turbulence is the adaptive challenge.

In nature, survival is not enough. Organisms that are merely surviving will die the moment the environment becomes a little challenging. To survive, you must thrive – this means a successful adaptation as well as developing the skills of adaptation. You can then handle challenge and stress by quickly developing a new adaptability in order to maintain yourself in that stressed environment.

In nature, there are three main tasks for adaptation: what DNA to keep; what DNA to discard; what innovations need to be developed to deal with the change around us. How DNA adapts provides an analogy for what leaders need to do today: leaders and organisations that wish to thrive in turbulent times need to be able to decide what should be kept, discarded, and created in order to evolve. It is worth mentioning, although it shouldn't need to be said, that this decision is not a once-off event!

To continue the analogy, a study done in 2002 by two marine biologists, Lance Gunderson and C.S. Holling, identifies four characteristics that make up the DNA of adaptive intelligence. They are helpful insights when it comes to understanding and applying adaptive intelligence to leadership in the corporate environment.

These four characteristics are:

1. **Learning to live with change and uncertainty.** This is an acceptance that the context in which we live and do business is one of constant change. A fixed rigidness and inability to embrace change and uncertainty militates against the development of adaptive intelligence. Of course, living with change and uncertainty is not easy and one way we cope is to make extravagant plans when it comes to the future. In a sense our plans are often nothing more than attempts to control the uncontrollable. They provide a sense of security that can be limiting when what we really need is an ability to hold lightly and move quickly. We will need to rethink the role and dependency on plans within our organisations. General Dwight D. Eisenhower said that 'plans are foolish but planning is essential'. Learning to live with change and uncertainty will mean that we need to understand what Eisenhower meant when he said that, and will require that we go about our strategic planning in a different way.

   Bob Johansen, in *The New Leadership Literacies* (2017), puts it very well: 'The future will reward clarity – but punish certainty.'

   Futurists tell us that at the moment, 80% of what tomorrow holds is what they term 'novelties'. In other words, the unforeseen – the unpredictable. Smart leaders recognise this and both model and build capacity within their organisations to live with change and uncertainty.

2. **Nurturing diversity for resilience.** There are several advantages that come with diversity – innovation for one, but another benefit that is not often recognised is that of resilience. What CEO doesn't believe that organisational resilience is important in today's climate? Of course, leading diversity is

tough. It requires a different mindset and skillset to what worked in the past, and the diversity that leaders face today transcends personal, cultural, generational, and structural boundaries. However, leading diversity is not optional, and so those in leadership need to build an awareness and acceptance of diversity that will ultimately lead to the development of resilience. Doing so requires new models and thinking and a willingness to learn from mistakes that will undoubtedly mark the journey. So important is this topic in the leadership agenda, we have added an entirely new chapter on the subject in this edition. So, we will speak more about this later.

3. **Combining different types of knowledge for learning.** This is where the collective failure of how we do leadership development/education/training is exposed. We still embrace the classroom experience as the dominant means of undertaking such learning, with the emphasis on information dissemination. It is estimated that some $50 billion is spent annually on leadership education/training/development, and yet in spite of this, the return on investment is questionable. Sadly, much of the current leadership pedagogy is stuck in traditional models or is being held hostage to academic ego and/or inhibiting institutional politics. We need to be bold in our willingness to try different things, and whether or not they work, there will be valuable lessons to be learnt. After all, there is not much 'proof of concept' of our current efforts to effectively equip leaders for tomorrow's world.

In teaching a strategic leadership class recently at one of South Africa's premier business schools, we were asked not to do an adaptive exercise essential to a deeper and practical understanding of Ron Heifetz's model of adaptive leadership.

The reason was that it was considered 'too risky', and the faculty concerned suggested that this was the client's request. Here's the problem: What if what we need to learn requires risk and a measure of discomfort? What if we don't know what we don't know? When the education process (actually, it is normally always a 'programme' rather than a 'process') is about 'pleasing the client', then questions as to what real learning is taking place have to be asked. A new world of work requires a new type of leader, and that in turn requires new approaches to leadership development.

4. **Exercising authentic leadership** in which adaptive intelligence is required demands that you be willing and competent at stepping into the unknown and stirring things up. 'Most people prefer stability to chaos, clarity to confusion, and orderliness to conflict. But to practice leadership you need to accept that you are in the business of generating chaos, confusion, and conflict, for yourself and others around you', writes Heifetz in his book *The Practice of Adaptive Leadership* (2009). This represents the polar opposite of what is often considered 'good leadership', and certainly his statement, and the thought it represents, demand serious consideration from those in leadership.

Becoming adaptive

So, how do we turn adaptive intelligence into a set of skills that can be applied? That's partly what this book is about – so keep reading. But maybe you'd like to start right now with a few practical ideas. In a lecture Prof Heifetz ran in Australia on adaptive leadership principles (see http://vimeo.com/13117695), he identifies the following seven behaviours of adaptive leaders:

1. **Conserving essential values and capacities** – recognising what is valuable and worth keeping, whilst adapting those things that need to change. Often, we make assumptions around what are the things worth keeping and what might need to change. It might be worth 'testing' this through some intentional discussion with your team as to what is worth keeping and what you regard as 'essential values and capacities'.

2. **Pervasive experimentation** – everything is open to trial and error investigations. Every company needs a 'sand pit'– a place where it is safe to experiment. To what extent is your corporate culture one of 'trial and error'?

3. **360-scanning for new challenges** – adaptive leaders don't wait for challenges to come to them – they go looking for them. This is not just formal 'environmental scanning' – it is a way of thinking rather than merely a process.

4. **Fast-paced, responsive improvisation** – requires taking a lifetime of experience and bringing it together to respond to unique new circumstances. 'Bringing it together' requires intentional processes – be those formal or informal. To what extent do you have such processes in place within your corporate structure or culture?

5. **Modelling of consistent, orienting values** – actually showing what values mean by their real-life expression is invaluable; wall-charts with lists of values mean nothing. 'Can you tell me some stories that illustrate how our values are being lived?' is a question leaders should ask of others throughout their organisation on a regular basis.

6. **Having a stomach for losses** – this means accepting that change will entail loss as well as gain, and that you have to move on from the past to create the future. Leadership is hardly ever a win-win game, and leaders have to make tough decisions – but also 'hold people tightly', with compassion and clarity, through the changes.

7. **Distinguishing leadership from authority** – when you have the know-how and a technical problem presents itself, then authority is all you need. But in an adaptive situation, you need leaders: people who know what to do when no one knows what to do. Importantly, you will need to engage all the stakeholders in finding a solution, and this will demand a different mindset and skillset from leaders. These new demands pose a real challenge to those leaders who are more comfortable with a 'command-and-control' style of leadership practice.

Our work at TomorrowToday Global leads us to add a few more practical items to his already helpful list:

8. **Seeking the right questions rather than the right answers** – too many leaders are trapped into thinking they must provide all the answers. Good adaptive leaders will ensure we're asking the right questions. They know the answers will change, but that if we have the right questions, we will continue to be able to keep up with these changing solutions. This book is intentionally full of questions, and one way to read it is to extract and make a list of every question posed throughout these pages. It is a list you can then add to with the input of those around you.

9. **Being comfortable with paradox – right-right thinking.** These leaders recognise that sometimes you have to choose

between a right and a right, and that sometimes there can be more than one solution. It's not about finding the win-win or compromise, but recognising that competing solutions exist, and then either choosing one or finding a way to hold them all in tension. Systems-thinking provides a helpful framework here.

10. **Embracing difference** – adaptive leaders actively seek to create environments of true diversity – unlike the environments we have now, which are often happy simply to create variety, but without pushing forward to an interacting ecosystem that is truly diverse. This is particularly important when it comes to putting teams together.

11. **Promoting dialogue and collaboration** – we need people from every part of an organisation to engage with adaptive problems, and not to wait for the authoritative experts to show them the way. We need leaders who create this type of environment. What is the conversation you need to have – but have been avoiding?

12. **Focusing on the need for self-organisation, emergence, and feedback loops** – this is a lesson taken directly from chaos/complexity theory. As a dynamic organisation adapts, it will often do so as a result of unpredictable forces, and much of the change will be unpredictable.

We cannot pre-programme the rules beforehand and anticipate every issue that might arise, and so we need to learn to lead and respond without dogged rules and regulations. Rather, we need processes of dialogue and engagement. Ideas, strategies, and actions will emerge as a result of generative dialogue. Rapid testing of ideas, strategies, systems, and actions – and then feeding back the results – will allow any person, team, or organisation to change direction and adapt to a changing context.

13. **Engaging in new ways of learning that are risky, uncertain, and messy** – almost all leadership and management development programmes are designed to be safe, to have predictable outcomes and consistent processes. As sensible and desirable as this might appear, it should be clear from what we say in this book that it may in fact inhibit what is really needed!

14. **Introducing future trends** – unless a futures context is developed, any strategy for any issue will be based on traditional tools of experience. Looking backwards and then extrapolating things forwards (basically the budgeting process!) can be very dangerous in preparing for the disruptive future. Although only demographics can be predicted with (some) accuracy, identifying future trends will allow those involved to build scenarios to better anticipate what impact these trends might have. It is vital to have as many people as possible involved in thinking about the impact of future trends.

15. **Being prepared to unlearn** – these leaders hold their truths lightly. Leaders who see themselves as being learnt might very well discover that what they know equips them for a world that no longer exists. We need leaders who are comfortable knowing that they are still learning.

Putting adaptive intelligence to work

Look over the list above and use it as a checklist or self-assessment.

Pay attention to habits as much as you do results and don't sacrifice the long-term for the short-term. Be patient but hold high standards. Give opportunity to participate and ask questions – lots of questions: of others, the organisation, and most importantly, of yourself. Be a learner and always believe there is a better way. Know the 'why' that underpins the 'what' and the 'how'; be intentional. Be suspicious of cookie-cutter approaches to leadership development. Be willing to allow open space in the learning process and look to build curiosity rather than certainty in both the programme and process. Be willing to fail and don't be afraid to model and champion the need to reflect. Invite the best from others and always believe that everyone has a contribution to make (and that they would rather make that contribution than not).

A quick 'tip' on habits: From neuroscience we learn that in our brain a habit is made up of a 'trigger' and a 'reward'. For example, a trigger might be having a cup of coffee, and the reward a muffin to accompany that coffee. To change a habit, we can either change the trigger or the reward. If there is a habit you have identified that you wish to change (or form), it might be helpful to identify and then think about it in terms of the trigger and reward associated with that habit and work from there.

This represents a start but – of course – not an end. The quest for authentic leadership and adaptive intelligence will be the hallmark of leading in the new world of work. Maybe this has always been the case.

Questions That Open Doors of Learning

Given all this, what methods or approaches will then work? If it is true that the mind works best in the presence of a question, then perhaps posing select questions will lead to finding out what methods and approaches might work best for you and your organisation. Here then are some questions to lead you to deeper conversations that will result in practical outcomes relevant to your particular context or theatre of leadership:

- If leading involves risk, what are the risks involved in teaching leadership?
- Can new insights move beyond conceptual awakening and actually change leadership behaviour at the level of default settings – habitual ways of responding, especially in crisis and under stress?
- If so, what are these 'new insights'?
- Who is the self that leads?
- What is your capacity for connectedness?
- What does 'leadership beyond technique' mean/look like?
- What is it about you that allowed great mentoring to happen?
- What does the 'learner leader' look like?
- What do you need to learn, unlearn, and relearn when it comes to leading in the new world of work?
- Are you an ethical leader?
- What would you do if you couldn't fail?
- What are you thinking/feeling about leadership but not saying?

5. Leaders Need to Be Future Focused

'Apres moi, le deluge.' King Louis XV

'Those who look only to the past or present are certain to miss the future.' John F. Kennedy

Louis XV was king of France just before the French Revolution. He reigned from 1715 (when he was only five years old) to 1774 (the Revolution fomented throughout the 1780s, eventually erupting in unrest on the streets in 1789). Wikipedia records that Louis XV is the king with the most ambivalent personality in the history of France. Much maligned by historians, modern research shows that Louis XV was in fact a very intelligent king dedicated to his task of ruling the largest kingdom of continental Europe. However, his indecisiveness, fuelled by his awareness of the complexity of problems ahead, as well as his profound timidity that was hidden behind the mask of an imperious king, account for the poor results achieved during his reign, and for the Revolution that followed.

The quote 'Apres moi, le deluge' is attributed to him. Roughly translated, it means 'After me, the deluge'. On one hand, it demonstrates a keen understanding of what was about to happen. But, more realistically, this quote is most often used to show how Louis XV, even though he knew what was to happen if the current system did not change, steadfastly refused to make the tough decisions required to bring about that change. Knowing that he could hold on to position and power throughout his reign at least, he essentially ran the French monarchy into the ground. It demonstrates the highest level of selfishness as a leader, focusing only on what happens during the leader's own tenure and caring nothing at all about what comes after.

The same is true of some leaders today. They run their companies (or schools, churches, synagogues, political parties, government departments, countries, country clubs, franchises, associations, charities, etc.) into the ground in pursuit of good short-term results (often in the form of a quick buck), with no thought or concern for what happens after they're gone. Maybe this is not even done consciously or deliberately, but it is nevertheless the outcome.

What happens after I've left

True leaders seek to be judged by what happens after they have left, not just what happens whilst they are there. When the celebrated Jack Welch left General Electric, after a quarter century of blistering results and being named *TIME* magazine's 'Manager of the Century', he reportedly told the media that they would only know if he was a truly great leader once his successor, Jeff Immelt, had been in the job a few years. Only then would we know how well he had prepared the next leader, and what shape he had left the company in.

How do we incentivise longer-term thinking? How do we ensure that leaders look beyond just their own tenures?

In Jim Collins's best-selling book *Good to Great* (2001), this is one of the key distinguishing factors of what he calls 'level 5' leaders: that they focus on building an enduring organisation that lasts beyond their tenure, rather than focusing on their own career and the company's success only whilst they are there.

We're not convinced that Collins fully understood this type of leadership. He doesn't do a great job in the book of explaining it or helping people to know how to attain it. But we do think he has discovered something important. In his research, his team identified five 'levels' of leaders:

- Level 1 is a Highly Capable Individual, probably acting in a solo, entrepreneurial capacity.
- Level 2 is a Contributing Team Member.
- Level 3 is the Competent Manager able to organise people and resources to accomplish a set task.
- Level 4 is an Effective Leader, usually leading by sheer force of personality, with an inspiring vision and ego to match, and focusing on high performance standards.
- Level 5 is the Executive who builds enduring greatness through a 'paradoxical blend of personal humility and professional will'; possessing great self-honesty, understanding, and emotional intelligence; keeping out of the limelight and setting up their successors for even greater success than they achieved themselves. (This is in stark contrast to the many 'celebrity CEOs' in the world of work at the moment.)

Fully developed leaders embody all five levels of leadership, and one does not need to develop from level 1 to level 5 in any sequence. Collins is convinced that level 5 leadership was a critical factor in every one of the 'good to great' companies his team analysed. But, as Collins himself points out, there is an inherent danger in the 'leadership is the answer to everything' perspective.

It's the modern equivalent of the 'God is the answer to everything' perspective that dominated the Dark Ages and held back scientific advancement. Before the Enlightenment, people ascribed all events they didn't understand to God. Why did the crops fail? God did it. Why did we have a bumper harvest this year? Praise be to God. Why did we have a tsunami? God did it. What makes the sunrise? God. Through the Enlightenment, we began the search for a more scientific understanding – physics, chemistry, biology, astronomy, and our various scientific pursuits.

Similarly, every time we attribute everything (either good or bad) to 'leadership' we're making the same mistake. We're simply admitting our ignorance. As Collins explains, 'Not that we should become leadership atheists (leadership does matter), but every time we throw up our hands in frustration – reverting back to "Well, the answer must be Leadership!" – we prevent ourselves from gaining deeper, more scientific understanding about what makes great companies tick.'

Part of the problem is that we do not design an entire system that supports and attracts the type of leaders we really need. Shareholders and boards of directors place immense pressure on senior executives to deliver on short-term goals, often at the expense of good strategic thinking. When you're judged each day by the daily closing price of your stock market ticker, it's no wonder good leadership seems so rare.

Executive remuneration also often militates against the emergence of level 5 leadership. How leaders are paid and earn bonuses can be a mystery, as companies that have posted serious losses regularly reward their CEOs and senior execs with bonuses in the same year the company loses millions. This outrageous practice causes an outcry and yet it continues to happen. The CEO's pay often bears no relation to reality at all – and therefore bears very little relation to demonstrated leadership.

The obvious starting point is to link senior executives' pay to actual company performance on a year-by-year basis. But even that would encourage short-term thinking. A much better solution would be to pay out bonuses to senior executives after they have left the company. In fact, it would make real sense to link the pension payments of retired execs to the ongoing performance of the companies they retired from. This would give real financial incentive for them to act like level 5 leaders whilst they have the reins of power.

However each organisation chooses to do it, the fact remains that it must be done – we must incentivise the right behaviour in our leaders. If we do not, it should be no surprise to us that, whether consciously or subconsciously, they are tempted to say, 'Apres moi, le deluge'.

Developing longer-term thinking

This then is the key to the type of leadership the world needs in the 2020s and 30s. It is a leader who looks to the future – not merely to predict what might change, but to develop a team and organisation that is ready for anything. And that can outlast them as leaders.

Although change has always been with us no matter what era we choose to focus on, it is the exponential rate at which it is accelerating at the moment that makes our era unique. The ability to change is, therefore, the most important of all leadership attributes.

For those invested in current models of leadership – be that the theory or the practice – the invitation to rethink remains unappealing for obvious reasons. But rethinking is precisely what we need to do. We need to be open to the fact that our leadership models, methods, practices, and paradigms need to change.

So, how then do we do this 'rethinking'?

On a personal level, there are three things you can do as a leader to ensure you cultivate the right habits and reflexes around rethinking. We will unpack these issues in more detail in the next three chapters, providing practical insights and ideas on how to develop them.

1. **Ask questions.** Start with yourself. Challenge your own assumptions and viewpoints. Start 'inside-out' with such questioning, but grow comfortable with being challenged 'outside-in'.

2. **Invite feedback.** Most leaders we know don't get the kind of feedback they need. It comes gift-wrapped in fear, politics, niceties, agreement, or endorsement. Authentic feedback is not given either because it is not invited, or because there isn't a safe environment in which 'real feedback' can thrive. Good and reliable feedback is the lifeblood of continued growth and fuels adaptation. Smart leaders intentionally create an environment that allows authentic feedback, and they don't exclude themselves from the feedback loop. Many leaders think they have achieved this when, in reality, they haven't.

3. **Know your biases.** We all have lenses through which we interpret the world around us. Understanding what these lenses are and how they impact on 'how we see' is the groundwork of emotional intelligence. We don't see the world as it is, but rather as we are. Furthermore, we lead out of who we are. This means that doing this 'inner-work' is simply not optional. As you learn to identify your own biases, it opens up the possibility of seeing differently – which, in turn, enables and energises the process of rethinking.

Through this 'rethinking', individuals and organisations will be able to recognise this new reality, but also intentionally develop coping mechanisms and skillsets that will help ensure that they don't 'miss the future'.

There is a thought-provoking Levi's advert that states: '*The future is leaving. Go forth*'. If you don't want to get left behind by the future, you will need to be able to rethink! So what might you (and your organisation) need to, as a matter of urgency, unlearn and rethink if you are to not be left behind? And how will you ensure that you build an organisation – and a team – that has a life long after you have left?

6. How to Change the World (by Asking the Right Questions)

'The art and science of asking questions is the source of all knowledge.'
Thomas Berger

'Those who change the course of history are usually those who pose a new set of questions rather than those who offer solutions.' *Gustavo Gutiérrez*

Nobel winning physicist and philosopher of science Richard Feynman said, 'I would rather have questions that can't be answered than answers that can't be questioned.' He was talking about the scientific method of investigating, developing theories, and verifying results. But he could have been talking about leadership.

Too many leaders see their role as being 'the person with the answers'. This is not surprising – most leaders are promoted to their positions on the basis of what they know, what they do, and being good at answering the questions that are asked of them. If the world is changing as much as we have suggested, then leaders need to change their thinking about their role. They need to realise that their answers don't matter if the wrong questions are being asked. It will be much better for leaders to shift from being question-answerers to question-askers.

This is not a small issue, nor just a play on words. Leaders are not that good at asking questions – genuine questions not designed to interrogate or produce a pre-programmed answer, but emerging from curiosity and a desire to know, discover, uncover, and illuminate.

In his book *21 Lessons for the 21st Century* (2018), Yuval Noah Harari put it this way: 'Questions you cannot answer are usually far better for you than answers you cannot question.'

We often don't welcome people who pose questions as they can be labelled trouble-makers, mavericks, and rebels. We have been conditioned to get rid of them, ignore them, or perhaps 'manage' them. They often make us feel uncomfortable, and they are not afraid to challenge the status quo, the conventional wisdom, and the formulae that to this point have brought success. They don't subscribe to the old cliché, 'if it isn't broken, don't fix it', and they are happy to ask and challenge, and are comfortable with being proven wrong. For them, 'asking the question' is what is important; finding the solution – that is entirely another matter, conversation, and perhaps, process.

If the truth be told, we have placed a far higher value on the 'solution' than on the question. We have been repeatedly told, 'don't bring me a problem; bring me a solution'. We are measured, valued, and rewarded on our solutions rather than on the questions we ask.

Yet history turns on great questions. If you are fortunate enough to have people in your team who ask questions, hang onto them and understand that their questions will enable you to find a 'better way', a break-through, a solution.

Questions engage, unlock, challenge, and reveal. Questions allow us to slow down or catch up. Used wisely, they are the weight that builds the muscle that leaders and organisations need if they are to make their way successfully into the future with all its inherent paradoxes, convergence, and complexity. Smart leaders understand that the time when 'leaders had all the answers' is long gone. They understand that their role is to be asking the right questions at the right time to the right people. That is not as easy as it may sound. In fact, smart leaders start by asking themselves questions that challenge their own certainties, assumptions, and viewpoints. An easy way to spot whether leaders do this is to see how they handle questions they are asked.

Three big questions

Really smart leaders know that the essence of leading in today's context is more about asking the right questions than feeling they always need to have the right answers. We are constantly surprised, however, by the gap that exists between what we hear from the CEO and from his or her people. When this discrepancy exists, it is because the leader has not found the answer to three important questions – the three questions that will help you as a leader gauge the health of your organisational culture.

Remember, there are two truisms concerning organisational culture: (1) culture is your responsibility, and (2) culture eats strategy for breakfast every time!

So here are the three questions you really need to be able to answer:

1. What are my people *really* thinking?

As the leader, it is important to know what your people are thinking. All too often leaders assume they know, yet the reality is that there is a gulf between what their people are really thinking and what leadership thinks they are thinking. This is of particular importance in any change initiative or process, and one cannot assume that what is being said reflects the real thoughts of your people. When there is a dislocation between what is being thought and expressed, there is cause for concern when it comes to your organisation's culture.

2. What are my people *really* saying?

All too often staff members merely parrot the 'company line' or express the 'safe' option rather than saying what really needs to be said. You cannot assume that what you hear your people say is what they are really saying. There are times when more is said by what is not being said, and smart leaders are quick to recognise this and respond accordingly. The presence of 360° appraisals and any number of performance review tools does not automatically translate into an open and transparent culture in which one can say what needs to be said. All too often these tools produce the exact opposite of that state. Smart leaders listen carefully and look for the cues to determine if what is being said is aligned with the true thoughts and feelings that underpin the verbal messaging that is taking place.

3. What are my people *really* doing?

It is said that 'actions speak louder than words'. All too often the actions (or non-actions) demonstrated by your people reveal that all is not well. Again, the measures we have in place can detect when this is the case – to a degree at least. There are actions that often fall outside the scope of such performance measures, actions that reveal the true state of affairs. Smart leaders are able to spot these, and they pay attention to any discrepancy in this particular expression of the organisational culture. How often have you heard the expression, 'don't do as I do, do as I say'? This highlights the discord that may exist, and when this type of statement is true of any environment, there is cause for concern.

They are simple questions, and for each question the key word is the *'really'*. What then can you, as a leader, do to reach the depths of these three cultural barometers? The simple answer is to 'walk the floor' in a manner appropriate to your particular context and culture. We know of a CEO of a private bank who abandoned his plush personal office and set up his desk in the middle of the open-plan space occupied by his staff. His reasoning was simply to be able to have an authentic answer to these three questions. This single act reverberated around the office in a manner that had a powerful impact on the organisational culture, and it remains one of the finest leadership examples we have ever witnessed.

To find the answers to these vital questions, you will need to look beyond the obvious and create mechanisms that will allow you to accomplish this. Make time for informal conversations; ask a lot of questions and then really (there is that word again!) listen; show up when you are not expected and participate in processes and activities that you wouldn't ordinarily be expected to be a part of. There are lots of creative ways to get to the heart of such questions – you just need to be disciplined enough to pause and think about how and what this could mean for you. It really is not that difficult. Right now you are most likely about to give the 'no time' defence. Our response to that is simply, 'really!'

Have you watched the reality TV series *Undercover Boss*? Each episode, the CEO of a company dons a disguise and goes to work in his or her own company posing as a new employee or intern. The CEOs spend time with frontline staff, and have eye-opening experiences at the business end of their businesses. Almost always they discover that things are not as they should be, or as the company policies and procedures manual outlines. And equally often they find deep insights into their organisations, industries, and people.

However you do it, there is perhaps no more important work or way in which you can spend your time than in knowing what your people are *really* thinking, saying, and doing. This is *your* responsibility!

Collecting questions

It is with this belief that we started collecting. Most people collect something or other. For some it is stamps, for others it might be model cars or antiques or things that have little significance beyond the passion of the collector. Our collection may be unusual, but it's also one every leader would do well to imitate, however presumptuous this may sound. It is not the kind of collection that one can display; nor is it one that could be sold as it really doesn't have any intrinsic value in and of itself. Yes, it is an unusual collection, but one we would like to share with you as you make your way in the journey we call 'leadership'.

We collect questions.

Not just any questions, but those kinds of questions that seem to have the ability to turn things inside-out, upside-down, and sometimes right-way up; the kind of questions that can serve as a companion for quite some time and that tend to stick with you, whether you like it or not; the kind of questions that are hard to ignore and the type of questions that somehow invite new insights and fresh perspectives; the type of questions that act as gateways to paths previously thought unattainable.

We have all encountered the magic of such questions: ones that seem to be carefully crafted for a specific time and place and that can change things forever when they intersect with our busy lives. They often take us by surprise and they don't come from a set template. They can appear innocuous, incongruent, and unpredictable when they show up.

Yes, good questions have the potential to move us forward. They have the potential to take us deeper, and when we understand that 'you lead out of who you are', the importance of finding the 'good questions' becomes obvious.

That's why we collect questions.

Some have been uncomfortable companions and others are still to be authentically engaged. Here then, for your consideration, are some of the questions that have made our list over the years. Some of them can only be asked of the individual, others can be asked of a team, organisation, or collective. Some simply need to remain private.

Why not write some of them down – those that resonate with you – and then start your own list? You will find questions suitable for yourself as well as those with whom you live and work. From the vantage point that we call 'hindsight', you won't regret starting this list. In no specific order, here are some questions from our collection:

- Have you found joy in your life?
- Has your life brought joy to others?
- Where is the place of your deepest learning?
- What do I want?
- Can I let go of that which I don't want to lose?
- What is the change that I am avoiding?
- What am I learning?
- To whom do I need to prove myself – and why?
- What can I learn from moments of embarrassment?
- What defines me?
- What makes me defensive – and why is this?
- What do I find in the silence?
- What in the silence finds me?
- What is the background music in my life?

- With whom or what am I competing?
- Where do I belong?
- Where did we come from?
- Who did we leave behind?
- Who are the guardians – and what are they guarding?
- Who are the paradigm shifters – and what are they saying?
- What do we/I need to learn next?
- What would be the most difficult thing for me to do this year?
- What am I avoiding?
- What gifts have I received?
- What is my gift?
- What is my trapdoor?
- What direction am I facing?
- What is the biggest risk I am facing now?
- What has been the hardest feedback I have received?
- What was 'the truth' in such feedback?
- When last did I receive feedback – what did I do with it?
- How would I like to be remembered?
- Why am I afraid to tell you who I am?
- What is our 'ridiculous' idea about our future?
- What would it take to realise this idea?
- What do we need to stop/start doing?
- Am I afraid of dying – why is this?
- Why should anyone be led by you? (*Also a great book by Rob Goffee and Gareth Jones, two London Business School professors.*)
- Why do you lead?
- What are you missing?

And one final question for you, the leader: *When last did you really ask a great question?*

7. The Lost Art of Reflection

'Reflection must be reserved for solitary hours; whenever she was alone, she gave way to it as the greatest relief; and not a day went by without a solitary walk, in which she might indulge in all the delight of unpleasant recollections.' Jane Austen

'Thinking is the place where all intelligent action starts.' Meg Wheatley

The practice of leadership has many important facets and nuances. Strategic formation and implementation are often regarded as the 'most important of all leadership responsibilities' and they certainly are important. Strategy almost always forms a core part of the curriculum in any leadership development programme. Leaders have become familiar with the models and tools associated with strategy; it is a subject that feels like 'leadership work' and is something that can be measured. Leaders tend to like that combination.

However, doing 'the work of leadership' does not necessarily equate to being a leader. When it comes to leadership, the 'doing' and 'being' agendas are very different. Over the years there has been a growing understanding and awareness of what leadership is and isn't – and how to go about the development of leaders. Keith's mentor and friend Dr Dudley Forde was well into his retirement years when he took on and completed his PhD in leadership – with a specific focus on education. We have learnt a great deal from Dr Forde through stimulating conversations facilitated by 'coffee meetings', as well as many hours of travelling together through our mutual work on some joint projects. The core of Forde's thesis was to review the evolving process that has characterised leadership education (we'll focus on that hot topic in chapter 14). Key to his findings is a missing element in leadership practice: reflection.

The theory of leadership has undergone many changes in the last century. Leadership theory initially led directly to leadership practice. At a Salzburg Global Seminar session Keith attended titled '*Linking the Theory and Practice of Leadership*', both leadership practitioners and academics were in attendance. It was a source of bemusement that the two groupings mixed as easily as oil and water! Whenever the practitioners were speaking of their problems and challenges, the theorists would mutter something along the lines of, 'Well, if you only paid attention to what we say and write, you would not be experiencing those problems'. Of course, when it came the turn of the theorists to share their insights and opinions, the practitioners in the room would roll their eyes and retort, 'Come and spend just one day in my office and let's see how your theories stack up!'

When the link in leadership was simply between theory and practice, the emphasis was on leadership as something 'you do', as a skillset to be mastered. And leadership was therefore seen and taught as a set of skills.

But like everything else in the scientific era, we wanted to find ways to measure leadership, so a third aspect was added to the 'leadership cycle': evaluation. Theory leads to practice, and practice in turn needs to be evaluated. This additional dimension introduced a plethora of evaluation tools, tools that today we simply take for granted. Evaluations became a standard part of 'best practice' and quickly became entrenched as part of any corporate environment. This has been the dominant framework for a long time: theory – practice – evaluation.

It is on the basis of this framework, for example, that agile methodologies have been created. The logic goes: what gets measured gets done, so the focus is on measurement and then working out what must be done and what development work is needed to enable people to do it. The same logic underpins management and leadership tools like balanced scorecards and 360 reviews.

The missing dimension

However, in recent times there has emerged a fourth element or dimension to the leadership cycle, one that 'closes the loop', bringing us back full circle to theory. The additional dimension is that of reflection: theory – practice – evaluation – reflection – theory...

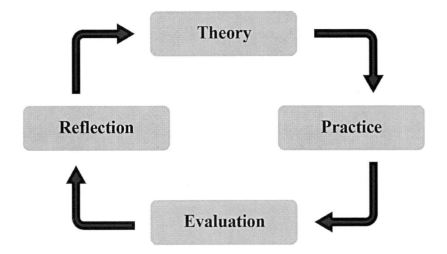

Source: Dr Dudley Forde

Reflection takes on many forms and descriptions. It can be seen as the habit of stepping back, or what the adaptive leadership model refers to as 'being on the balcony'. It can be seen as the pause, the space to think before taking action. Margaret Wheatley, author of *Leadership and the*

New Science (1999), describes the act of thinking as the thing that precedes all intelligent action or activity. Thinking, and taking intentional time to think, are not necessarily the same things – certainly not in the corporate world where 'taking time to think' is not understood and seldom practiced.

We once worked with a CEO who decided that he needed to practice the disciplines of reading and thinking in a way that was visible at work. This decision emerged from a conversation we had following an article we wrote titled, 'If you are too busy to read; you are too busy'. He decided that every day he would spend seven to ten minutes at his desk reading a leadership book. One day as he was doing so, a colleague walked into his office apologizing for interrupting him, then seeing he was reading added, 'Oh, so you're not busy then…' and proceeded to engage the CEO. The CEO commented that this reaction was insightful: reading was considered something to do 'if one wasn't busy'. He decided there and then that he needed to challenge and change this perception and culture within his team.

This 'new' element (reflection) to the leadership cycle has introduced another dimension to the leadership discussion – that of 'being'. It is an understanding that the leadership agenda is no longer merely about 'doing', but it is also about the character ethic. It is an understanding that you 'lead out of who you are' and that whilst skillsets are important, they are no longer the definitive element in leadership development and practice. Aristotle referred to great leaders as being 'great souled', and West Point (the US Military Academy) prioritises character development in their leadership approach above all else. This is why leadership development cannot be confined to a programme but needs to be seen and approached as a lifetime pursuit. Much of this remains unfamiliar to those in leadership, or at least, if known, it remains viewed with suspicion and a fair degree of scepticism.

We do have some sympathy for this take on the subject given how poorly this 'new agenda' is often positioned and presented. Hard-nosed and cynical leaders have little time and less patience for some of the extremely poor attempts and efforts to raise their awareness in this area. It is often reduced to the 'motivational' agenda and left to external speakers and consultants, who are viewed as anything from 'entertainment' (motivational speakers) to an 'unnecessary evil' (consultants), or to hacks who practice disconnected and uninformed forms of meditation and mindfulness (gurus).

Reflection requires practical tools and clear articulation as to the 'why', 'what', and 'how' if it is to gain traction within our corporate organisations. In a global context of increasing complexity, connectedness, and volatility, finding time to think is not only challenging but a necessity.

So can leaders 'do' this essential work?

Of course, there are no easy answers, but there are some important practical steps to consider:

- Understand that the approach to the discipline of reflection will be strongly nuanced by 'who you are'. Some find it relatively easy to be still and pause in the moment without an overwhelming need to 'do something'. For others, this practice is extremely difficult. Acknowledging your own bias in this area will be an important platform from which to build a reflective habit as a leader.
- Start by scheduling specific time (20 minutes a few times a week might be a realistic initial target) to step back and spend a set time reflecting. You can keep these periods short, but having them scheduled into your routine will help ensure that they take place. Do your level best to honour this

'appointment' and if you cannot (as will happen), then reschedule that 'lost' time. Doing so will help ensure that it isn't permanently deleted. This discipline will go a long way to building the reflective habit.

- Pick a time and location that will afford you the best opportunity to be reflective.
- Start by deciding how best to use this time. You could read, journal, scribble notes around something that will be the focus of your reflection, or merely sit still and think. Being 'busy' during a reflection can end up serving as a distraction, one that actually keeps you from the discipline itself. But for busy types, having 'something to do' is a good start, and over time you can wean yourself from such activities and get more comfortable with the truer forms of the reflective practice. There is a lot of helpful material on the subject, and exploring various resources and finding out what works best for you is all a necessary part of the journey.
- Determine to 'stick with it' for a good period of time (at least two months) before stepping back and reviewing how you are doing, what the benefits might be, and what needs to happen next. You need to allow this important work to become habitual in order to secure the true benefits on offer. Developing a sustainable reflective practice as a leader is essential to 'leading out of who you are'.
- Investigate mindfulness. Much has been written about this essential topic, and you can find a variety of approaches that will suit your personality and profile.

No longer will a focus on efficient operational expertise and an over-reliance on experience be enough. Leaders will need to step back, step out of, and consider the disruptive influences, connect the dots, and see the big picture. They will have to become comfortable with asking good questions and being able to harness the wisdom and perspective of the many. They will be required to rethink and revisit many of the formulae and methodologies that have brought success in the past – an unlearning process that is often as traumatic as it is difficult. They will need to think like futurists.

Building reflection into how we develop leaders

When those responsible for leadership education and leadership development programmes (LDPs) understand the need for reflection as part of both leadership theory and practice, we suspect that many of these programmes will come to look very different (more of this in chapter 14). There will be a greater emphasis on self-awareness and an unpacking of what it means to 'lead out of who you are'. Time will be made for reflection and pauses will become more commonplace. It will change some of the work expected and done; it will alter the metrics – the 'what' and 'how' we measure; it will both look and feel different. This is something of what the emerging mindfulness movement is attempting to achieve.

This is why some of the ways things are done will no longer apply. Despite the insistence of some leading business schools on grading reflective papers set for the LDP participants, we cannot see how this can actually be achieved. How does one actually grade a reflection paper?

Here is an example of one such paper. The instruction was simple: select any aspect of what you've experienced in the past few days of this course and reflect on its significance for you. No further detail or instruction was given. As the papers rolled in, we found it amazing to discover the general tenor that underpinned the exercise. A general response to the assignment was summed up by expressions like: 'life changing', 'the most important work I have done in years', and 'why has it taken so long for me to do this kind of work'. But some participants took the opportunity to reflect on some of their deepest valleys in life – burying a child, the death of a spouse or parent, divorce, growing up in grinding poverty, having abusive parents, and so it goes on. Reading these papers often makes one feel like removing one's shoes as you are 'standing on holy ground'. It is an immense privilege to have such personal narratives shared, and the insights and leadership lessons that are made are often profound.

But how does one grade such stories?

Certainly there can (and should) be comment on effort, approach, and engagement with the tough and demanding work that is reflection... but a grade? There needs to be the encouragement to see this essential discipline as part of a leadership practice that will eventuate in it becoming a leadership habit, but ascribing a grade to it is just too simplistic and is entirely the wrong thinking.

But that is what is expected in academia. That is what is expected in a LDP. You grade, you mark, you compete with the person next to you, and you strive to come top of the class. But when it comes to the deep work of reflection, these mindsets make no sense. In fact, not only do they make no sense, they often do harm. The same is often true in business itself. Reflection needs to bring immediate business benefit or 'results', or it is quickly abandoned as a waste of time.

In the development of leaders, when it comes to the character ethic, the emphasis on emotional intelligence, and the growth of self-awareness, certain things cannot and should not be graded or measured by traditional measures. But try making the business schools and CEOs see this! And so this is why, as the leadership agenda shifts in the context of a changing world and the new world of work, so many current 'successful' models will fail to deliver.

We should be teaching leaders to think, to adapt, to reflect, to unlearn and relearn, to question, to pause, and to explore inwards as well as outwards – but we don't. The tools that will deliver on many of these things remain too edgy, too 'unscientific', and yes, are not measurable.

So we stumble on, afraid to change the curriculum, afraid to make mistakes, and sometimes afraid to stand up to those who don't always know best what they need. We continue as we were, only with smarter technology, slicker programmes, and more subject experts; yet in spite of such efforts and investment, we fail to see any meaningful change in both mindset and behaviour.

The fact is that someone has to lead this new charge to reshape our approach and thinking on leadership. The reality is that it will come from different sources from a variety of settings. Embracing it and adopting it into your context will be the work of leadership. It will be culturally nuanced as much as it will be driven by personalities. It will look different from place to place and will need to be used differently from setting to setting. However, the ability to reflect, at both an individual level as well as at a corporate level, will be an essential survival tool for 21st-century leadership and living.

A good place to start might be with your executive or management team. What would a reflective habit look like in the mix of your meeting agendas and daily routines as leaders?

We know of a CEO of an engineering firm, for example, who at our suggestion introduced a time of silence to 'bookend' his executive agenda. Each meeting was started and ended with a period of silence. Initially greeted with real scepticism by his team, this practice has grown to become an essential part of their executive meeting, with telling results. You might need to be bold. In fact, you will need to be bold, given the prevailing conditions. You also will need to be willing to try some things that may not work. However, as with getting physically fit, it will take time, perseverance, discipline, and effort. But, as with getting fit, it will become easier with time and the benefits will be felt and seen by all.

You want to be 'future fit'? Well then, we suggest incorporating reflection as a discipline towards that goal. We don't think you will regret doing so.

8. Flat-Earth Thinking, and How Leaders Can Combat It

'To know that we know what we know, and to know that we do not know what we do not know, that is true knowledge.' Nicolaus Copernicus

'It isn't what you don't know that gets you into trouble but what you know for sure that just ain't so.' Mark Twain

On 16 February 1600 a crowd had gathered to watch the Italian friar, philosopher, mathematician, and astronomer Giordano Bruno being burnt at the stake. To go against the 'truth', as the Church defined it, was to run the risk of being labelled a heretic, which was his fate.

His crime? Following on the work of Nicolaus Copernicus, who had advanced the heliocentric view of the universe, Bruno had proposed 'new truths' about the universe and how it worked at a time when the Church believed the earth was the centre of the universe. A few years later, the great Galileo Galilei would be tried by the Inquisition for the same heliocentric views and forced to recant and spend the last decade of his life under house arrest. Of course, we now know that Galileo, Bruno, and Copernicus were on the right path in believing what they did, but that counted for little when stacked against the prevailing status quo – the 'truth' of the day.

At the time, most people considered the earth to be the centre of the universe, and the common conception was that it was flat as well (although, of course, educated people had moved beyond the flat-earth theory). When the flat-earth and geocentric perspectives ruled, those who first suggested alternative realities were considered deranged and, in some quarters, heretics; considering what punishment lay in store for heretics, this would almost certainly have been enough to make one think twice before going against the grain! Copernicus valued his life enough to officially hold back his views (his book was literally published on the last day of his life in 1543), and Galileo felt obliged to recant his views about heliocentricity. Not so for Bruno, and look at what happened to him.

We call the inability to look for new truths 'flat-earth thinking'. Calling out contemporary flat-earth thinking still carries with it a stigma and exclusion, and may even, in extreme circumstances, still possess a life-threatening menace. Certainly it is likely to have career-inhibiting consequences, and as a result there seem to be few willing to run the risks involved in challenging current 'wisdom' and the prevailing worldviews, whatever they may be.

However, it is a great question to be considering: What constitutes flat-earth thinking in how we are going about seeing and doing things?

We would highly recommend you read *Uncommon Sense, Common Nonsense* (2012) by Jules Goddard and Tony Eccles – it's one of the best books on this topic in the last decade.

Flat-earth thinking flourishes when the current dogma goes unchallenged. Dogma is 'perceived truth', and therein is the rub. When I (we) think we have a corner on the 'truth', what is there to debate? One of the more important leadership responsibilities is for leaders to identify such thinking and be able to lead their organisation away from the precipice that inherently comes with a flat-earth belief. This is easier said than done. The forces invariably opposing any new thinking have marshalled in their corner the majority, the status quo, and conventional wisdom. It is a formidable array of weaponry to have at one's disposal!

There are three key approaches to developing new thinking: recognise your own cognitive bias, identify blind spots, and give up the belief that you always are – or need to be – right. Let's look at these issues:

Cognitive bias and how to combat it

Cognitive bias occurs because the human brain perceives and processes information through a filter of personal experience and preferences, causing errors and prejudice in our thinking and conclusions. We are typically unaware of these errors in thinking because our brains fool us into thinking we have all the information we need and have processed this information in entirely consistent, coherent, and logical ways. Sadly, this is almost never the case – our brains prioritise and process the vast amount of input received each second by taking shortcuts, summarising, and even manipulating what we perceive.

Daniel Kahneman, in his brilliant book *Thinking, Fast and Slow* (2011), provides many examples of cognitive bias – one is particularly frightening. He studied hundreds of parole hearings, looking for evidence of bias in whether the parole board approved the prisoner release or not. He discovered that prisoners who had their hearings immediately after a refreshment break were 65% more likely to be released, whereas those whose hearings came just before a coffee or lunch break were never successful in their hearings. This is a truly horrifying piece of information. There is no way that the judges would be aware of this bias – if they were, they would surely immediately deal with it. The bias is unconscious. And it is very, very real. (Note to self: if you ever find yourself in court, do everything in your power to avoid the before-lunch time slot.)

This actually happens all the time in our daily lives. We tend to trust our brains, our intellect, and our reasoning abilities – very few people go through life second-guessing their judgment all the time. People who do, don't end up as leaders, let's be honest. In leaders, we value decisiveness, confidence, resolve, and assuredness.

And yet, every single person who studies the brain and how it works warns us that our brains trick us all the time. Modern neuroscience confirms that our senses should not be trusted, and that our brains lie to us and trick us on an ongoing basis, in issues big and small, important and irrelevant.

Take our memories, for example. In a series of episodes of his superb podcast *Revisionist History*, author and social researcher Malcolm Gladwell deals with the issue of memory (see http://bit.ly/gladwellmemory). He uses the example of a massive study of people after the 9/11 attacks in New York in 2001. Within a few days, researchers interviewed thousands of people asking them to recall where they were when they heard about the attacks and to give details of what they were doing. Participants wrote these accounts down in their own handwriting.

Ten years later, researchers met up with these people again and asked them to recall the events of that day. Many people had very different memories of what had happened. When they were shown their original written memories, they often disputed these, rather trusting their own current memories than the handwritten evidence from 10 years earlier. They were adamant their memories were accurate, even though it was obvious to everyone except themselves that they were not.

It is easy to understand why: if we cannot trust our memories, life is very difficult to deal with. None of us wants to believe that we can't trust our memories. Or indeed, our reasoning skills in general.

But this is what science tells us: our memories are almost all wrong. Or at the very least, distorted. Our brains trick us all the time.

Great leaders in the 2020s and beyond need to admit this and deal with the consequences of accepting what this means for how we engage with the world and with other people around us. It is beyond the scope of this book to provide you with a detailed analysis of cognitive bias. We encourage you to take time to read about this and train yourself to identify and combat as many cognitive biases as you can. Identify which cognitive biases are most likely to impact you, given your industry, role, and personal profile.

What we can do is briefly outline the most significant cognitive biases that we see playing out day after day in offices around the world:

1. **Confirmation bias**. This is the tendency to look for or interpret information in a way that confirms existing beliefs. If you believe something, your brain immediately embarks on the task of confirming that belief. Whenever you come across evidence that your belief is correct, your brain flags this, stores it, and assigns high value to it. If you come across evidence that contradicts your belief, your brain ignores this, discounts it, and gives you reasons to reduce the value of the evidence. We reinforce our ideas and attitudes by selectively collecting evidence or retrieving biased memories. We need to work really hard to combat confirmation bias – it is exceptionally powerful.

2. **Recency, availability, and anchoring biases**. When trying to make a decision, we have a tendency to focus too much on a single piece of information rather than all available information. This usually happens with the first piece of

information you received (anchoring bias), the most recent information you received (recency bias), or the most emotional information you received (availability bias).

3. **Framing bias**. The way a problem is framed strongly influences the subsequent choices we make. The way we ask questions can have a significant impact on the answers people give. This is because people tend to accept the frame they are given, seldom stopping to reframe it in their own words, or examining (and rejecting) any premises that are contained in the way the question was asked.

   Consider, for example, if your team tells you that an activity they're attempting has a 1 in 5 chance of success, or if they say it has an 80% possibility of failing. Which of these scenarios *feels* more acceptable? You know they're exactly the same, but it sounds more ominous that something has an 80% chance of failure. If your team wants you to approve it, they'd be better off framing their request as a 1 in 5 chance of success.

We overcome these biases by being aware of them and putting deliberate strategies in place to counter them. Name them, know them, recognise them, protect against them, and deal with them. For a full list of cognitive biases, and links to resources for each, see: http://rationalwiki.org/wiki/List_of_cognitive_biases.

Identifying our blind spots

Decoupling or 'disenthralling' ourselves from our favourite methodology, pet theories, or well-worn traditions that have outlived their usefulness and purpose is never easy. Yet this is what the work that challenging flat-earth thinking entails. In furthering this discussion with a client from a major law firm, he added a valuable insight into why it is that dogma is so difficult to let go of or to challenge: 'It becomes dogma because you live it. You don't choose it at the outset, it becomes such over time, as you come to defend it and so start to live it', he said. He is right.

There are three things that leaders can utilise to counter flat-earth thinking.

1. **Curiosity**. The enemy of dogma – of flat-earth thinking – is curiosity. The presence of curiosity will always mean that things that are taken for granted will be challenged. Children are born curious, but then as they enter formal education the natural gift that is curiosity is educated out of them. Educator Ken Robinson has a wonderful TED Talk on the subject (http://bit.ly/KenRobTED), and it is hard to argue with his point that we in fact steer our children away from their inborn curiosity in the pursuit of educational objectives. Smart leaders look to nurture and foster curiosity within the DNA of their organisations. Smart leaders understand that well-directed curiosity can lead to wonderful things and so they actively encourage it, believing there is always a better way to do things.

   Here might be an interesting exercise for you to conduct: at your next team meeting, count the number of questions asked without telling the participants what it is you are doing. It might be worth recording the actual questions asked and then categorizing and evaluating them. Questions for the sake of questions aren't always helpful. Learning how to pose the 'right' question is an art that needs developing. This might take time but one has to start somewhere in the quest for quality questions as a natural ingredient in your meeting mix. Oscar-winning Hollywood producer Brian Grazer describes in his book *A Curious Mind* (2016) how he has spent a lifetime conducting 'curiosity conversations'. It is a practice he initiated as a young man and has persisted with throughout his career. It involves first identifying select people – anyone from whom he has something he wants to learn. He then doggedly pursues getting an audience with them, to ask them the question he has framed. It is a wonderful way to combine curiosity, questions, and learning. If you have a team that you suspect is no longer learning, why not hold them accountable to just one curiosity conversation per month? Then ensure that these are shared in your meetings, and give the process time to deliver insights and learnings and to build the habit of curiosity.

2. **Courage**. If you are going to be curious, courage will be required. Courage means that you are willing to live with the consequences of where your questions and subsequent actions might lead you. Courage means you are not prepared to play the political games that characterise many work environments. Courage means that you are willing to be wrong; that you value authenticity; that you take a stand. Courage demands values – values that serve to anchor your curiosity and that provide reassurance to others who choose to follow you into unchartered territory.

3. **Commitment**. Leaders need to be committed to the process that challenging flat-earth thinking will require. We live in work environments dominated by programmes and quick fixes. There is often little appreciation or patience for things that require process. Commitment means an appreciation for processes and the willingness to see things through – even though it may take time and no small amount of effort. To challenge prevailing wisdom and turn that into a new way of

seeing/doing/being is seldom instantaneous or done easily. Disruptive processes are the lifeblood of innovation and newness, and what such processes look like requires wisdom, perspective, and... commitment.

More great questions and actions for leaders

Practically speaking, how can these concepts of curiosity, courage, and commitment be added to your leadership toolkit? Here are some pointers on how best to cultivate these three 'weapons' intentionally in the war against flat-earth thinking.

- Ask questions that start with 'why'.
- Challenge assumptions.
- Don't be afraid to initiate a 'pause' in meetings to think some more.
- Start your meeting with a period of silence – and take note of the responses.
- Look to learn from failure. Suspend judgment and interrogate the entire process that led to the failure.
- Read biographies of those you deem to have been courageous and committed. Share their stories with your team.
- Define what you mean by 'committed'. Answers might surprise you depending on the age of the respondent!
- Watch children at play... then go and play with them. Allow them to be 'the boss' of whatever it is you are engaged in.
- Journal.
- Watch movies/TV programmes that you might not ordinarily watch.
- Take a different route to work every day for a week.
- Rearrange your office. Do without your office.
- Look to learn something new every week. Keep a record of your learning.

- Invite others to perform functions that you usually reserve for yourself. Watch how they go about it.
- Take the youngest/newest/oldest/most maverick members of your team/staff to lunch and ask them questions about what they think/see/feel when it comes to working in your team/company.
- Identify the urgent things driving your agenda. Then list the things that are important. Discuss your findings with someone you feel might be able to reflect with you/offer some helpful perspective.
- Read the Dr Seuss book *Oh, the Places You'll Go*.
- Ask five good customers/clients what you could do differently in your dealings with them – things that would enhance the relationship or add value. Now do the same with five customers/clients who you would rather not have that conversation with!
- Ask your team (individually) to hold you accountable for something that you want to improve concerning how you lead.
- Explore the Enneagram as a personal assessment tool/framework.
- Find/meet with a mentor.
- Identify people you think are curious/courageous/committed and try to get to know them better.
- Watch the sunrise/sunset every day for a week.
- Identify what the most courageous thing you have ever done was and then reflect on the circumstances, results, and impact of that event/moment. What insights do you take from this for where you are today?
- Volunteer to help out at a charity/non-profit for a short period of time.
- Invite yourself to dinner with a staff member who is from a different culture/background from you.

- Walk the floor; visit places in your office/factory that you seldom get to.
- Do somebody else's job for a morning/day.
- Ask 'is there a better way' for at least five things in which you are routinely involved within the context of your work/leadership. Explore the options.
- Suspend some rules/restrictions in the 'way things are done' in your company and see what results.
- Ask five people for the 'best book' they have read – and read them. Make sure at least two are fiction.
- Ask people what is important to them concerning their work. Don't settle on the first thing (or even the second thing) they tell you. Dig deeper.
- Ask others in your organisation questions like, 'If you had my job, how would you go about doing it? What might I be missing? What do you think we have in common?'
- Commit to having at least six curiosity conversations with a variety of individuals. Document the process and insights. Challenge someone on your team to the same task.

We think you get the point. If we were to pause more regularly and ask questions like these and engage in activities like these, it would have the effect of creating greater innovation, providing clearer insights, and allowing us to move forward more confidently. It might serve to enhance the debate, even change the debate and free us from getting stuck as we so often do when it comes to contentious issues.

Now to take this further: select seven things from our list (one for each day next week), add seven further things of your own, and then start doing them. Start actions that will nurture habits and see where that takes you. Some of what you elect to do may be private, others you may want to share – or even invite participation.

This type of 'stuff' isn't really that hard. It is just that many leaders neglect it... and then forget about it altogether, and the trap of flat-earth thinking is sprung without them even knowing it!

Always right?

This is further exacerbated by the expectation in flat-earth thinking that the leader should be, or is, always right.

Of course, getting more things right than wrong as a leader is good and something that anyone in leadership would strive to achieve. However, this isn't the same as being right all the time. The problem is that many in leadership believe that their perspective, their experience, their solution is the right one. When this is the overriding approach, it means that other options automatically are relegated and subjugated to the leader's 'right'.

When leaders are 'right' (all the time), it usually means that an autocratic, command-and-control leadership culture prevails. It quickly becomes a toxic context in which others don't speak up and one in which participative decision-making and innovative solutions are suffocated. 'Right' means that there can be no room for other considerations; 'right' means that there is no room for discussion and debate; 'right' means that we stop looking around and focus only on what we are told is in front of us and apply only what has been determined.

This is not the context of collaborative and participative environments. Leaders who insist on their 'right' usually means that the benefits delivered by diversity get ignored as the wisdom of 'the many' is sacrificed for the wisdom of 'the one'.

There can be no discussion with anyone who believes that they are right. Any discussion is really nothing other than an arm-wrestle around 'right-wrong' rather than an authentic exploration to find a new perspective and embrace new learning. There is a Sufi saying that goes, 'beyond the field of right and wrong is a place; I'll meet you there'. Anyone who has had the misfortune to engage in a 'discussion' with a fundamentalist (of any persuasion) will know immediately the futility of such a 'discussion'. Fundamentalists believe that they are right. They refuse to – or are unable to – put aside 'their rightness' to create room for meaningful engagement. Such conversations quickly degenerate into angry exchanges and invariably damaged relationships.

There are people for whom 'right and wrong' defines their approach and shapes their worldview. Such a person has a far longer road to travel when it comes to meeting at that 'place' that the Sufi saying speaks about – the place that sits beyond the field of right and wrong. For others, those who are able to entertain paradox and who are comfortable negotiating the 'grey' of life, access to that 'place' is far easier.

Leaders need to see how their 'right' inhibits free discussion and stunts dialogue. Smart leaders know how and when to suspend their 'right' in order to allow a 'better way' to emerge. Leaders who remain unaware of how limiting and overbearing their 'right' has become are a danger to the organisation and those they lead.

But are we suggesting then that there is no 'right'?

Of course not.

In various scenarios there is a strategic right, a moral right, and an obvious right – it is just the mindset involved that will determine how others are allowed to influence, persuade, contribute, and challenge. Recently, whilst in Singapore, Keith had lunch with a federal New

York judge who told him, 'As a 5'3" woman, I could never bully anyone. I have had to find ways to get others to co-operate, agree, and go along with me my entire life.' We are sure, like us, you know people who are 'always right'. People who are certain about so many things – things that any thinking person would immediately recognise as having an antithesis, a counterpoint, an opposite.

Beware of your right – your right may be a dogma. It may even be modern-day flat-earth thinking. As a leader, catch yourself in discussions where you hear yourself proclaim the right; be mindful of thinking habits which revolve around 'right and wrong' and be willing to explore further, to venture beyond – in order to find 'that place'. As a leader, help others find that place beyond right and wrong. As you do so, know that it will significantly contribute to an organisational culture in which opinions are respected, learning is prized, and participation leads to both accountability and an 'ownership' for realising the desired objectives.

Being right is a trap of flat-earth thinking, but it need not be. Whether or not it is a trap, well… that will be up to you.

Take a moment

We've just finished three chapters on three key new skills for leaders: asking questions, reflection, and knowing your biases.

We are about to suggest a model of leadership that will make sense of the new world we live in.

We need you to pause for a moment to consider the enormity of the change we're proposing in a model for leaders. We're not asking you as a leader to simply free up a few minutes in your otherwise manic diary to try and squeeze a few more items onto a to-do list. We're not saying that there are a few new skills to add to your toolkit and then everything will be OK again.

We're suggesting that there needs to be a fundamental realignment of what leaders are expected to do, how they are expected to behave, how we should follow them, how we should measure – and reward – their contributions, and what they should focus their time, energy, and resources on.

Too many leaders are caught up working IN their businesses and not ON their businesses. Not enough leaders are working ON themselves either. They're glorified managers, making the odd future-focused decision. They consider themselves 'top of the pile', 'king of the hill', 'commander-in-chief'. But, in reality, they're not leading. Not in a way that will bring success in times of deep, structural, and disruptive change anyway.

It will take boldness, courage, effort, and commitment to become the type of leader we're proposing. And it won't be without its risks, or its detractors.

Pause here for a moment.

If you are keeping a journal as you read this book, go back over what you've written so far and see whether it accurately reflects the enormity of the shift we're suggesting.

Whether or not you're keeping a journal, take some time now on a blank page to list the potential dangers and downsides for you personally of embracing the type of leadership model we're proposing. You need to appreciate the cost that will have to be paid to develop into the type of leader that can truly lead in a changing world. We know it won't be easy, and counting the cost is therefore an important part of the journey – or even the decision to embark on the journey at all.

When you've done that, also take a while to reflect on these leadership thoughts:

'It ought to be remembered that there is nothing more difficult to take in hand, more perilous to conduct, or more uncertain in its success than to take the lead in the introduction of a new order of things. Because the innovator has for enemies all those who have done well under the old conditions, and lukewarm defenders in those who may do well under the new. This coolness arises partly from fear of the opponents, who have the laws on their side, and partly from the incredulity of men, who do not readily believe in new things until they have had a long experience of them.' *Niccolò Machiavelli*

'I want to be in the arena. I want to be brave with my life. And when we make the choice to dare greatly, we sign up to get our asses kicked. We can choose courage or we can choose comfort, but we can't have both. Not at the same time.' *Brené Brown*

'If your actions inspire others to dream more, learn more, do more, and become more, you are a leader.' *John Quincy Adams*

'Education is the most powerful weapon which you can use to change the world.' *Nelson Mandela*

'Vision without action is merely a dream. Action without vision just passes the time. Vision with action can change the world.' *Joel Arthur Barker*

'Before you are a leader, success is all about growing yourself. When you become a leader, success is all about growing others.' *Jack Welch*

'What would you do if you weren't afraid?' *Sheryl Sandberg*

'I wanted to change the world. But I have found that the only thing one can be sure of changing is oneself.' *Aldous Huxley*

'A man who wants to lead the orchestra must turn his back on the crowd.' *Max Lucado*

'Use your life to serve the world, and you will find that it also serves you.' *Oprah Winfrey*

Pause.

Continue…

A Definition of Leadership?

Whole forests have died to print the mountain of paper on which definitions of leadership have been written. Think about how often you've had a discussion about the difference between leadership and management by way of example of this.

For most people, the definition of leadership comes down to something like 'getting work done through other people'. There's something deeply disturbing about this view. Let us explain why.

Picture two different bosses engaging with a staff member. Boss A says, 'The task you're trying to complete is something I did for a living more than 10 years ago. What I did worked and I was good at it. I'll show you how to do it, and then I want you to do it that way.' (They may add extra instructions like, 'Shut up', 'Don't ask any questions', and 'You don't need to even think about it. Just do it my way.' Whatever their exact words, you get the picture.)

Boss B says, 'The task you're trying to complete is something I did for a living more than 10 years ago. What I did worked and I was good at it. If you think it will help, I'd be happy to show you what I did.'

Which boss would you rather work for?

Of course, Boss B is seen as the better boss. Boss A doesn't feel nice at all. But there's something more profound going on here than just people dynamics, communication style, and emotional intelligence.

Look at these two bosses again, and think of the situation in terms of the means and the end (the process and the outcome). In front of both bosses is a task that needs to be done and a person. For Boss A, the end result is the completion of the task, and the means to achieving this is the person. The person is simply a 'human resource', a means to an end. And we've already established this doesn't feel good – at least not for the staff member.

For Boss B, it's the total inverse: the task is the means, and the person is the outcome. The development of the staff member is the focus. In the way Boss B phrased the initial statement, we have an invitation – an invitation to partnership, an invitation to engagement, an invitation to development. But also the option to decline the invitation. There is also an acknowledgement of the possibility that the way Boss B completed the task a decade ago may not be the way it should be done today.

Now here's the rub. If leadership is defined as 'getting work done through other people', which boss best demonstrates this approach? It's actually Boss A, isn't it? Boss B is 'getting people done through work'. Sounds strange – but read that again. Boss B is *getting people done through work*. Changed and improved people are the focus and desired outcome. The task at hand is merely the way in which this is achieved.

This is actually what we believe leadership is about. Leaders use the work that must be done as the 'excuse' to develop their people.

Leadership expert Etsko Schuitema distils this thought to a simple essence that he calls the Care and Growth Leadership Model. Leaders that you want to work for do two things, he says: **they care for you and they help you grow**. Nothing less. Nothing more.

- Take some time to evaluate whether you are more like Boss A or Boss B.
- You probably are a blend of those two caricatures, so it might be more helpful to ask yourself under what conditions you are most likely to act like Boss A.
- In what ways does this set a negative tone for your team?
- How can you become like Boss B?

We actually have an answer for that last question: *become an invitational leader*.

The next few chapters will introduce you to this model of leadership and outline some key skills to help you do just that.

9. A New Model of Leadership:
The Invitational Leader

'Too many people separate the act of leadership from the leader. They see leadership as something that they do – rather than as an expression of who they are. If we want to be more effective with others, we need to be more effective with ourselves.' Kevin Cashman

'No one should be considered educated to lead without understanding that leadership is relational.' Barbara Kellerman

If leaders need new approaches that are adaptive and take account of the paradoxes of 'right-right' thinking, then an entirely new model of leadership will be valuable. Just like the explorers of the past who set sail for unknown lands, so too today's leaders may have to set their sails to catch new winds. In her dynamic book *Leadership and the New Science* (1999), Margaret Wheatley likens attempts to chart the future as similar to that of the explorations of those early sea adventurers whose maps and accompanying commentary were 'descriptive but not predictive, enticing but not fully revelatory. They pointed in certain directions, illuminated landmarks, warned of dangers, yet their elusive references and blank spaces served to encourage explorations and discoveries by other people... they contained life-saving knowledge, passed hand to hand amongst those who were willing to dare similar voyages of their own.' This is where we find ourselves now with leadership models.

Newton's world

The current leadership models within our organisations and institutions with which we are familiar are grounded in a particular context referred to as the 'Newtonian' worldview, shaped primarily by the genius of Sir Isaac Newton and French philosopher/mathematician René Descartes during the course of the 17th century. In essence, Newtonian thinking held that the world was like a machine, the whole made up by the parts. To understand the machine, one only had to remove the individual part, examine it, and replace it; so too to fix it. It was this framework/worldview that informed the Industrial Revolution (see chapter 3 above), which in turn paved the way for our contemporary organisational hierarchies, establishing the 'rules of the game' in so far as leading organised work is concerned. This represents a gross over-simplification of events and influences that have led us to our current context but are sufficient for the purposes of this book.

Newtonian thinking led organisations to champion the twin towers of control and predictability – marshalling their energy and resources accordingly. In this context, leadership evolved to be something that was always 'at the top', always visible, controlling, strong, and the place where the buck stopped. The desired state was one of equilibrium and stability, achievable by imposing control, constricting people's freedom, and inhibiting local change. The system in which this took place would be described as a closed system. This was a system where information was controlled and chaos and change were minimised.

It is noteworthy that nature has taught us that the attempt to manage for stability and to enforce an unnatural equilibrium always leads to far-reaching destruction. In essence (and ironically), managing for stability threatens the very system itself.

Quantum worlds emerging

However, as explorations into the subatomic world gathered momentum from the early part of the last century, a growing dissonance with

Newtonian thinking emerged. The 'rules of the game' that held true in the Newtonian universe collapsed in the subatomic world being explored. The subatomic world offered a new landscape of connections and paradox, of phenomena that could not be reduced to simple cause and effect, or explained by studying the parts as isolated contributors. The early pioneers of quantum theory, Niels Bohr and Werner Heisenberg, found that at the end of each question they asked in an atomic experiment, nature replied with a confusing paradox.

Growing out of this new understanding emerged an alternative worldview, one that provides some critical reference points for the way in which we view organisations and leadership. For one thing, there appeared to be a fundamental connectedness in this new order that refuted the matter/persona dichotomy of the Newtonian worldview. A physicist, J.S. Bell, proposed a theorem in 1964 (which was confirmed experimentally in 1982 by Alain Aspect at the University of Paris) that proved that the world is fundamentally inseparable. In other words, that matter could be affected by non-local causes and be changed by influences that travel faster than the speed of light. University of California, Berkeley physicist Henry Stapp has described Bell's theorem as 'the most profound discovery in the history of science'. We are not sure how this connectedness works, but there is a certainty that there is 'separation without separateness'. Nothing can be understood in isolation; everything has to be seen as part of the unified whole.

What we are discovering in the world of physics helps us make sense of some of what we're seeing in society around us too, and in our organisations (especially the large multinationals that become complex ecosystems in themselves). Wheatley makes the point that we have broken the world into parts and fragments for so long that we are not well prepared to see that a different order is moving the whole. Finding new ways to think about, to see, sense, and comprehend the whole represents one of the greatest challenges for today's leaders. Understanding this connectedness has vast implications for our constructions of organisations and leadership, now and into the future. Future leadership will be built on epigenesis: the formation of an organism out of genetic and memetic characteristics rather than generic principles, but one that advances in complexity of form and structure. ('Memes' is a term first coined by Richard Dawkins and refers to culturally transmitted ideas and customs that have been implanted in the human brain by social interaction and historical development.) In this regard there is much we can learn from cultures such as the Native Americans (the Circle of Courage), the Japanese (the concept of 'Kyosei'), or the African spirit of 'ubuntu' as it is interpreted and practiced by different groupings. There is a common nervous system we all share.

Learning to view the whole system is difficult. Ricardo Semler, in his book *Maverick* (1995), states that every organisation should pay somebody to 'look out the window'. However, our traditional analytic skills can't help us in this quest as analysis only serves to narrow our field of awareness and actually prevents us from seeing the whole system – the panoramic view. Seeing the big picture is reliant on work involving the whole group. Wheatley makes the point that as people engage together to learn about their collective identity, they are able to see how their personal patterns and behaviours contribute to the whole. This then empowers them to take personal responsibility for changing themselves.

This type of 'collective inquiry' is reflected in the Quaker practice of the 'Clearness Committee' and has some important lessons for leadership in the new paradigm. Leaders need to be able to see what they are doing as they are doing it; this is where the true learning is. Author Scott Peck refers to this as the ability to 'metamood'. (*Metanoia* comes from a Greek word meaning a 'fundamental shift of mind'.) To develop this 'observer self' requires patience, practice, and no small amount of curiosity. This provides the raw materials from which to fashion the tools that enable the leader to deal with diversity. Dealing with diversity is a challenge inherent with open systems and a prerequisite of future leadership. Leaders can't deal with the challenge of diversity because someone has told them along the way that it is 'the right thing to do'. Leaders embrace diversity because of how they 'see', and how they 'view' the whole, coupled with a fundamental belief in people.

Chaos, it now appears, is a vital and necessary ingredient in the process of change, change which leads to a higher evolution. It is chaos's great destructive energy that dissolves the past and gifts us with the future. This is true at both the personal and organisational level. When we concentrate on individual moments or fragments of experience, we see only chaos. However, when we stand back and look at what is taking shape, we see order. Ancient myths and new science both teach that every system that seeks to stay alive must hold within it the potential for chaos. As organisational author T.J. Cartwright frames it, 'Chaos is order without predictability' ('Planning and Chaos Theory'). Stacked against this reality, the leader who tries to control and ensure a predictable, chaos-free environment is heading for a leadership abyss.

Coming to terms with this on a personal level is essential before living it out as a leader. Of course, both are a never-ending process. Simply put, leadership into the future, without a willingness to engage in the often-painful work of interior excavation and soul-searching, will not withstand the shift or change in paradigm and worldview. Danish philosopher Søren Kierkegaard said, 'To venture causes anxiety, but not to venture is to lose one's self... And to venture in the highest is precisely to be conscious of one's self.'

The invitational leadership model

We therefore present a venture into a new model of leadership, based on the concepts of invitational theory. This theory is embedded in an educational context, but has found resonance for leaders in every sector of society all around the world.

The term 'invitational' was chosen for its special meaning. The English *invite* is a derivative of the Latin word *invitare*, which means 'to offer something beneficial for consideration'. Translated literally, *invitare* means to 'summon cordially, not to shun'. Implicit in this definition is that inviting is an ethical process involving continuous interactions amongst and between human beings.

Invitational theory is a collection of assumptions that seeks to explain phenomena and provide a means of intentionally summoning people to realise their relatively boundless potential in all areas of worthwhile human endeavour.

It is based on two successive foundations: the 'perceptual tradition' and the 'self-concept theory'. These two foundations, each supported by decades of scholarly research and writing, provide invitational theory with both substance and structure.

In applying invitational theory, a most important question is, 'What is the fit amongst perceptions of various individuals?' *The perceptual tradition* maintains that human behaviour is the product of the unique ways that individuals view the world. The perceptual viewpoint places consciousness at the centre of personality. It proposes that people are not influenced by events so much as their perception of events. The perceptual tradition was beautifully presented in the 1962 Yearbook of the Association for Supervision and Curriculum Development, *Perceiving, Behaving, Becoming*, edited by A.W. Combs.

A second important question in applying invitational theory is, 'Who am I and how do I fit in the world?' This question derives from the second foundation of invitational theory: *self-concept theory*. Self-concept is a complex and dynamic system of learnt beliefs that each person holds to be true about his or her personal existence.

The theory maintains that behaviour is mediated by the ways an individual views himself or herself, and that these views serve as both antecedent and consequence of human activity. Out of these views, four assumptions emerge that present the 'character challenge' for invitational leadership and provide the personal raw material from which purpose, direction, and behaviour can best be shaped.

The four assumptions are: *trust, respect, optimism,* and *intentionality.*

Trust

Human existence is a co-operative activity where process is as important as product. A basic ingredient of invitational theory is recognition of the interdependence of human beings. Attempting to get others to do what is wanted without involving them in the process is a lost cause. Given an optimally inviting environment, each person will find his or her own best ways of being and becoming. Invitational leaders require a degree of trust that the process will produce the result they're seeking, and that the individuals involved in the process are all committed to producing positive results.

Respect

People are able, valuable, and responsible and should be treated accordingly. An indispensable element in any human encounter is shared responsibility based on mutual respect. This respect is manifested in the caring and appropriate behaviours exhibited by people, as well as the places, policies, programmes, and processes they create and maintain. It is also manifested by establishing positions of equality and shared power.

Optimism

People possess untapped potential in all areas of human endeavour. The uniqueness of human beings is that no clear limits to potential have been discovered. People are works in progress, their best selves often still unrealised. As Michelangelo famously said of his David sculpture, he just kept chipping away everything in the marble that was not David, until the image itself was revealed.

In his book *Synchronicity: The Inner Path of Leadership* (2011), Joseph Jaworski states that 'leadership is all about the release of human possibilities'. For invitational leaders, optimism regarding human potential is not an option; it is a prerequisite. It is not enough to be inviting; it is critical to be optimistic about the process. No one can choose a beneficial direction in life without hope that change for the better is possible. From the standpoint of invitational theory, seeing people as possessing untapped potential determines the policies established, the programmes supported, the processes encouraged, the physical environments created, and the relationships established and maintained.

Intentionality

Human potential can best be realised by places, policies, processes, and programmes specifically designed to invite development, and by people who are personally and professionally inviting with themselves and others. An invitation is defined as an intentional act designed to offer something beneficial for consideration. Intentionality enables people to create and maintain total environments that consistently and dependably invite the realisation of human potential.

The four essential principles of invitational theory – *trust*, *respect*, *optimism*, and *intentionality* – offer a consistent stance through which leaders can create and maintain an optimally inviting environment. Whilst there are other elements that contribute to invitational theory, these principles are the key ingredients.

Applying invitational leadership

What then would be the possible application areas for such leadership? There are at least five areas that exist in practically every environment, all of which can contribute to the success or failure of every leader. In the same way as everyone and everything in hospitals should invite health, so everyone and everything in every setting should democratically and ethically invite the realisation of human potential.

These five areas are people, places, policies, programmes, and processes. These five 'Ps' make up the 'ecosystem' in which individuals continuously interact and in which leadership occurs.

Whilst everything in life adds to, or detracts from, success or failure, nothing is more important in life than *people*. It is the people who create a respectful, optimistic, trusting, and intentional society. In the past, much of leadership was seen to have to do with accomplishing certain tasks, achieving predetermined goals, regardless of the people concerned. The invitational leader consciously and consistently invites others to participate in creating their own future, giving them the space and opportunity to do so. It has been said that no person on their deathbed wishes they had spent more time at the office. During the course of 2001, Keith had the privilege of being a travel companion of a friend dying of cancer. Days before his death, I asked him what had been the greatest insight he had received as a result of his illness. 'The importance of relationship' was his immediate answer. An invitational leader leads with this awareness, even when called on to make tough decisions and see a task achieved.

The physical environment (*places*) offers a practical starting point for invitational leadership because places are so visible. Almost anyone can recognise smelly restrooms, cluttered offices, peeling paint, or unkempt buildings. Fortunately, places are the easiest to change because they are the most visible element in any environment. They also offer the opportunity for immediate improvement.

Policies refer to the procedures, codes, and rules, written or unwritten, used to regulate the ongoing functions of individuals and organisations. Ultimately, the policies created and maintained communicate a strong message regarding the value, ability, and responsibility of people. The invitational leader constantly questions and invites the review of these policies to ensure they serve the current environment and needs and are working towards what is trying to be achieved. Stories of policies that are intended to serve the customer/client but which accomplish the exact opposite are, of course, legend in customer care training.

Programmes have an important part to play in leading in an inviting way because programmes often focus on narrow objectives that neglect the wider scope of human needs. For example, special programmes that label people can give individuals ideas about themselves that negate the positive purposes for which these programmes were originally created. Open system leadership uses networks; Newtonian mindsets still rely on boxes. Invitational leadership requires that programmes be monitored to ensure that they do not detract from the purposes for which they were designed.

The final P, *processes*, addresses the ways in which the other four Ps function. From the early Greek philosopher Heraclitus to the most recent thinking in science, life has been described as a process. Process looks 'backstage', at the forces behind what is seen on the stage of life itself. Processes address such issues as co-operative spirit, democratic activities, collaborative efforts, ethical guidelines, and humane activities. They focus on how the other Ps are conducted. It is the role of the invitational leader to be the 'gatekeeper' but not sole custodian for the processes at work within his/her organisation. Although we see change at the material level, processes that are immaterial invariably cause the change. The invitational leader learns to develop a sixth sense for these invisible processes, rather than the things they engender. Learning to live in a process world that defies employing a 'methodology' to cope with such a reality is a challenge for the invitational leader.

This requires a role-change for leaders. A change from being the 'master creator/controller' to one that is willing to participate in the 'dance of life'. It is an invitation to hear the music and then dance! Henri Nouwen, in his book *Clowning in Rome* (2001), plays on the metaphor of the circus, suggesting that the movement needed for authentic leadership is to go from being (or trying to be) the highly admired and skilled trapeze artist who performs high above everyone, and who requires people to crane their neck in order to catch a glimpse of the breathtaking stunts, to being the clown. The role of the clown in the circus context is one with which we can so readily identify and with whom we are invited to share both their tears and laughter.

It is useful here to contemplate the complexity of invitational theory. Many people think they already understand the concept of 'inviting'. They see it as simply doing nice things – sharing a smile, giving a hug, saying something kind, or buying a gift. Whilst these may be worthwhile activities when used caringly and appropriately, they are only manifestations of an invitational stance one takes. This invitational stance determines the level of personal and professional functioning.

Levels of engagement

The following levels provide a check system to monitor each of the five Ps (people, places, policies, programmes, and processes) that are found in and around any human endeavour and that reflect invitational leadership in action.

Intentionally uninviting

The most negative and toxic level of human functioning involves those actions, policies, programmes, places, and processes that are deliberately designed to demean, dissuade, discourage, defeat, and destroy. Intentionally uninviting functioning might involve a person who is purposely insulting, a policy that is intentionally discriminatory, a programme that purposely demeans individuals, or an environment intentionally left unpleasant and unattractive.

Unintentionally uninviting

People, places, policies, programmes, and processes that are intentionally uninviting are few when compared to those that are unintentionally uninviting. The great majority of uninviting forces that exist are usually the result of a lack of an invitational stance. Because there is no philosophy of trust, respect, optimism, and intentionality, policies are established, programmes designed, places arranged, processes evolved, and people behave in ways that are clearly uninviting, although such was not the intent.

Individuals who function at the unintentionally uninviting level are often viewed as uncaring, chauvinistic, condescending, patronising, sexist, racist, dictatorial, or just plain thoughtless. They do not intend to be hurtful or harmful, but because they lack consistency in direction and purpose, they act in uninviting ways. Leaders who function at the unintentionally uninviting level may not intend to be uninviting, but the damage is done. Like being run over by a truck: intended or not, the victim is still dead.

Unintentionally inviting

People who usually function at the unintentionally inviting level have stumbled serendipitously into ways of functioning that are often effective. However, they have difficulty when asked to explain why they are successful. They can describe in loving detail what they do, but not why.

An example of this is the 'natural born' teacher. Such a person may be successful in teaching because he or she exhibits many of the trusting, respecting, and optimistic qualities associated with invitational theory. However, because they lack the fourth critical element, intentionality, they lack consistency and dependability in the actions they exhibit, the policies and programmes they establish, and the places and processes they create and maintain.

Leaders who are unintentionally inviting are somewhat akin to the early barn-storming airplane pilots. These pioneer pilots did not know exactly why their planes flew, or what caused weather patterns, or much about navigational systems. As long as they stayed close to the ground, followed a railway track, and the weather was clear, they were able to function. But, when the weather turned bad or night fell, they became disoriented and lost. In difficult situations, leaders who function at the unintentionally inviting level lack dependability in behaviour and consistency in direction.

The basic weakness in functioning at the unintentionally inviting level is the inability to identify the reasons for success or failure. Most people know whether something is working or not, but when it stops working, they are puzzled about how to start it up again. Those who function at the unintentionally inviting level lack a consistent stance – a dependable position from which to operate.

Intentionally inviting

When individuals function at the intentionally inviting level, they seek to consistently exhibit the assumptions of invitational theory. Author Jean Mizer described how schools could function to turn a child 'into a zero', presenting a beautiful example of intentionality in action (*Cipher in the Snow*, 1964). Mizer illustrated the tragedy of one such child, then concluded with these words: 'I look up and down the rows carefully each September at the unfamiliar faces. I look for veiled eyes or bodies scrounged into an alien world. "Look, Kids", I say silently, "I may not do anything else for you this year, but not one of you is going to come out of here a nobody. I'll work or fight to the bitter end doing battle with society and the school board, but I won't have one of you coming out of here thinking of himself [*sic*] as a zero."'

In invitational theory, everybody and everything adds to, or subtracts from, human existence. Ideally, the factors of people, places, policies, programmes, and processes should be so intentionally inviting as to create a world where each individual is cordially summoned to develop physically, intellectually, and emotionally. Leaders who accept the assumptions of invitational theory not only strive to be intentionally inviting, but once there, continue to grow and develop, to reach for what is referred to as the 'Plus Factor'.

When people watch the accomplished musician, the headline comedian, the world-class athlete, the master teacher, what he or she does is made to seem so simple. It is only when people try to do it themselves that they realise that true art requires painstaking care, discipline, and deliberate planning.

At its best, invitational theory becomes 'invisible' because it becomes a means of addressing humanity. To borrow the words of Chuang Tsu, an ancient Chinese philosopher, 'it flows like water, reflects like a mirror, and responds like an echo'. At its best, invitational theory applied to leadership requires implicit, rather than explicit, expression. When leaders reach this special plateau, what they do appears effortless. Football teams call it 'momentum', comedians call it 'feeling the centre', world class athletes call it 'finding the zone', fighter pilots call it 'rhythm'. In invitational theory it is called the 'Plus Factor'. A good example of this factor was provided by Ginger Rogers when describing dancing with Fred Astaire. She said, 'It's a lot of hard work, that I do know.' Someone responded: 'But it doesn't look it, Ginger', to which she replied, 'That's why it's magic.'

Invitational leadership, at its best, works like magic. Those who function at the highest levels of inviting become so fluent that the carefully honed skills and techniques they employ become invisible to the untrained eye. They function with such talented assurance that the tremendous effort involved does not call attention to itself.

Personal and professional

Invitational leadership encourages individuals to enrich their lives in each of four basic dimensions: (1) being personally inviting with oneself; (2) being personally inviting with others; (3) being professionally inviting with oneself; and (4) being professionally inviting with others. Like pistons in a finely tuned engine, the four dimensions work together to give power to the whole movement. Whilst there are times when one of the four dimensions may demand special attention, the overall goal is to seek balance and synchronicity between personal and professional functioning.

Being personally inviting with oneself

To be a beneficial presence in the lives of others, it is essential that invitational leaders first invite themselves. This means that they view themselves as able, valuable, and responsible. They exhibit trust, respect, optimism, and intentionality towards their own actions and attitudes. They are the kind of leaders who remain open to new experiences and who adopt a positive learning attitude throughout their entire life. These leaders see the need to reinvent and renew themselves on a regular basis, and take the opportunities and develop the disciplines to do so. Hopefully you now understand how some of what we've been talking about already in this book underpins the experience of an invitational leader.

Being personally inviting with oneself takes an endless variety of forms. It means caring for one's mental health and making appropriate choices in life. By taking up a new hobby, relaxing with a good book, exercising regularly, learning to laugh more, visiting friends, getting sufficient sleep, growing a garden, or managing time wisely, people can rejuvenate their own well-being. Much is currently on the shelves in the leadership section of bookstores on precisely this aspect of leadership. It is well documented from a variety of standpoints that without being inviting with oneself, it is not possible to be truly and authentically inviting towards others.

Being personally inviting with others

Being inviting requires that the feelings, wishes, and aspirations of others be taken into account. Without this, invitational leadership could not exist. In practical terms, this means that the social committee might be the most vital committee in any organisation.

Specific ways to be personally inviting with others are simple but often overlooked. Getting to know colleagues, sending friendly notes, remembering birthdays and significant anniversaries, enjoying a staff social, practising politeness, being vulnerable, and celebrating successes are all examples of invitational leadership in action.

Being professionally inviting with oneself

Being professionally inviting with oneself can take a variety of forms, but it begins with ethical awareness and a clear and efficient perception of situations and oneself. In practical terms, being professionally inviting with oneself means trying a new method, seeking certification, learning new skills, returning to graduate school, enrolling in a workshop, attending conferences, reading journals, writing for publication, and making presentations at conferences.

Keeping alive professionally is particularly important because of the rapidly expanding knowledge base. Perhaps never before have knowledge, techniques, and methods been so bountiful. Canoes must be paddled harder than ever just to keep up with the knowledge flood.

Being professionally inviting with others

The final dimension of invitational leadership is being professionally inviting with others. This involves such qualities as treating people as individuals, not as labels or groups. It also requires honesty and the ability to accept less-than-perfect behaviour of human beings.

In everyday practice, being professionally inviting with others requires careful attention to the policies that are introduced, the programmes established, the places created, the processes manifested, and the behaviours exhibited. Amongst the countless ways that leaders can be professionally inviting with others are to have high aspirations, fight sexism and racism in any form, work co-operatively, behave ethically, provide professional feedback, and maintain an optimistic stance.

Leaders who combine the various dimensions of invitational theory into a seamless whole are well on their way to putting the theory into practice.

In summary, the major components of Invitational Leadership are:

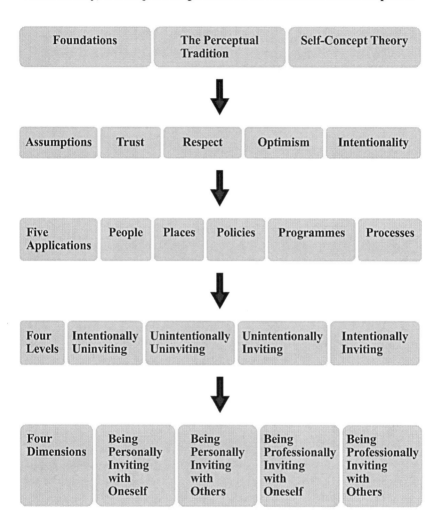

| Foundations | The Perceptual Tradition | Self-Concept Theory |

| Assumptions | Trust | Respect | Optimism | Intentionality |

| Five Applications | People | Places | Policies | Programmes | Processes |

| Four Levels | Intentionally Uninviting | Unintentionally Uninviting | Unintentionally Inviting | Intentionally Inviting |

| Four Dimensions | Being Personally Inviting with Oneself | Being Personally Inviting with Others | Being Professionally Inviting with Oneself | Being Professionally Inviting with Others |

Concluding thoughts

Invitational leadership is the intentional invitation to others to participate in/create their own future, a future that is connected. For those placed in positions of leadership, the challenge is there: the leadership of the future ought to be the leadership of your present! Confucian philosopher Meng Tzu said, 'If the King loves music, there is little wrong in the land.' Leaders will need to actively recognise and embrace invitation and participation as the way to lead into the future, confident that as they do so, and untidy as it certainly will be, 'little can go wrong in the land'.

Reflective Exercise

This has been something of a 'deep dive' into the underpinning structures that provide us with the powerful invitational leadership model. The real work for you as a leader is to build practical behaviours on the invitational foundation. Consistent and influential leadership practice always has sound foundations, and so before reading further, it might be appropriate to pause at this point and think through what invitational leadership could look like in your own sphere of leadership influence.

- How could you translate the invitational leadership model (philosophy) into daily actions and activities?
- What would invitational leadership look like in your environment?
- What aspects of invitational leadership make immediate sense to you, and which are slightly puzzling or confusing?
- What does this say about your current leadership paradigm?

As a reflective exercise, you might want to consider these questions, relooking at the basic principles of invitational leadership (trust, respect, optimism, and intentionality) and explore how you can live each of these out in your leadership practice.

Take another moment

The next five chapters are each an invitation to rethink a critical aspect of your leadership approach and practices in the light of what has been said about adaptive and invitational leadership. Before you proceed, take a moment to list the five most important aspects of your own leadership that you feel you need to work on or rethink.

If you are keeping a journal, make these notes there; otherwise, use the rest of this page to jot down your thoughts...

1.

2.

3.

4.

5.

10. Leading Difference Differently: An Invitation to Rethink Diversity

'It is not our differences that divide us. It is our inability to recognise, accept, and celebrate those differences.' Audre Lorde

Difference matters. Most corporates today fully acknowledge this with significant investments ploughed into the area tagged 'diversity and inclusion' – an area that extends from personnel to programmes. The 'rules of engagement' have been well articulated and are firmly in place, and yet we still have a problem. Politeness now stands in the way of authentic and meaningful engagement. In an arena that is dynamic and complex, leaders are all at sea when it comes to how to engage with the topic and what to do.

This inescapable and increasingly frenetic cacophony around the issue of diversity or difference is not going to go away. It will dominate leadership discourse for years to come in much the same way that the subject of innovation has been inextricably coupled with any leadership conversation or programme. Issues around race and ethnicity, gender, age, sexuality, class, and many other 'categories' dominate the news and media. The 'issues' are surfacing everywhere, from politics to the corporate world, from communities to the everyday 'normal', mundane interactions. The dramas both real and imagined are noisy, newsworthy, and impossible to ignore. They are symptomatic of a deeper and more pervasive issue running through our contemporary societies that are interwoven by the ubiquitous threads of social media.

Of course, this is hardly a new issue. Prejudice and discrimination is as old as human history. The compass points of yesteryear, pointing enticingly to far-away places, have increasingly converged; what was once an imaginative stretch is now within a short reach as societies, and all that is inherent within them, are not only accessible but collide with jarring frequency. A prejudice once hidden by distance and/or ignorance is now easily made more explicit. What was once avoidable, or could be justified and rationalised in some distorted way, is now simply an ever-present reality that refuses to be placated by the old and defunct explanations. The subject demands our attention; it is both a foundational stone as well as a capstone to all of our futures.

What should be of deep concern though is the alarming failure of the many past interventions to make a difference in this area. There has been a battery of attempts to highlight and deal with diversity, a concerted bombardment that seems to have yielded little return and, in some cases, may even have made things worse! Our best efforts have resulted in a 'political correctness' that having initially helped with awareness and behaviour now acts as a straightjacket to conversation and limits meaningful and authentic engagement. It is a constraint that we don't seem to know how to free ourselves from, and any attempts to do so appear clumsy and often yield deeper offence and hurt. 'I simply don't ask anymore', one frustrated senior executive said to us when it came to dealing with difference within his work environment, 'because if I do, it invariably just leads to trouble.'

In many instances, 'diversity and inclusivity training' – as it has been tagged – is met with a resigned sigh and a numbing participation as something that 'needs to be done' and 'got out of the way' as quickly as possible. There is an unspoken acceptance that nothing will really change as a result of our best efforts. Our initiatives merely add to the veneer covering the subject, glossing over it without us having to actually deal with it, but at least we can tick it off as 'done'. Somehow the irony is that our best efforts have made engaging with diversity (or what we prefer to simply call 'difference') even more inaccessible. The topic is fast reaching a point of burnout and fatigue that has rendered our well-intended efforts counterproductive.

Why is this?

It is because we have failed to understand the real core of the problem: *ourselves*. We have looked at addressing the subject from entirely the wrong standpoint and our approach, whilst good 'on paper', has failed to impact the real 'on field' behaviour. We have looked to put in place stringent rules to govern the on-field behaviour but failed to recognise that something more, something fundamental, and something deeper needs to be addressed.

To meaningfully engage with difference is to start with 'me'. Before looking at those 'out there', we first need to confront the person 'in here'. The starting point for dealing with difference is to acknowledge our own biases and prejudices. It is to start with identifying and understanding the lenses through which we see and interpret the world around us. The reality is that we don't see the world as it is but rather as we are.

Allow us to use ourselves, the authors, to illustrate this point: We are both *white, male, South African, older generation (Baby Boomer/Gen X)*. These are merely four (of many) 'lenses' through which we try to make sense of the world, and each, in its own way, radically impacts on 'what it is I see'. To believe any differently would be naive at best and intentionally stupid at worst. If we are to begin to see differently, then we have to first ask how these inherent biases impact what we look at, notwithstanding other powerful undertows such as religion, education, socialisation, and context.

In dealing with difference, we have started at the wrong place. Whilst there is evidence of some progress, by and large we have not got to where we need to be.

This is, and always has been, personal work – inner landscaping if you like – and this type of work is largely alien to our formal learning structures and pedagogies. To do this essential work, we need authentic processes, not stand-alone programmes; we need time and space, not the clipped and formatted schedules; we need subtle guides and givers of context, not tick-box managers and 'experts'; we need qualitative descriptors and not meaningless metrics; we need community and interdependence where we all understand what is at stake and what is the endgame, rather than mere efficiencies and 'functional teams'. In short, we need to rethink much of our entire approach to this subject if, that is, we want a different outcome.

It will require both massive revisions and bold and courageous individuals (and organisations) to expose the limitations and shortfalls of our current endeavours. We know this, but someone has to be willing to take the lead and pioneer what really needs to be done, even if they don't fully know how best to do that work or where exactly it may lead. Beethoven's philosophy to music was to go 'beyond knowledge' – to explore the territory 'beyond the script or score'. The danger here, of course, is that this unchartered territory means uncertain outcomes and surprising destinations. But this is where we need to go if we are to unlock the full benefits and meaning of difference; this is where we need to venture if we are to understand what we don't understand and learn what it means to use our differences to be different together.

Our society is fragmented, angry, and in disarray. To some extent this reality gets muted when 'society' walks into our respective 'places of work', where a different set of rules are observed and certain behaviours expected. However, this only serves to dull the noise and deflect the inescapable issues that remain.

So let us come back to the place where we started and make some clear and bold statements for your consideration that hopefully might serve as a catalyst for some action.

1. The challenge of leading difference will be the predominant leadership challenge of the immediate future. It is work that needs to be done in order to unlock the real and obvious benefits of harnessing difference.

2. This essential work is, at another level, work we all have to do. The leader's responsibility is to create an environment where this work is permissible and possible, and you (as a leader) need to be willing to demonstratively lead the way in doing the necessary work.

3. We need to acknowledge that our best efforts to this point in time simply haven't worked. In many respects dealing with difference is an adaptive challenge that has been treated and approached with a technical mindset. A fundamental revision is needed by those tasked with the wonderful responsibility of educating, developing, and training. It will take bold and courageous educators to challenge the current status quo and modus operandi of educational institutions tasked with preparing people to lead. Until we develop formal programmes and processes to engage this work in a meaningful way, we will have more of the same without making any real progress. Some of the required work will entail giving permission to experiment (and possibly fail) with a willingness to change the design and metrics of our traditional and current programmes; we will need to know what to keep, discard, and create in order to develop leaders capable of leading difference effectively. *(As an aside, we know for a fact that there are many good and capable people within these learning institutions eager to engage in this work and contribute towards something more meaningful and sustainable. The obstacles blocking their way are not insurmountable.)*

4. Engaging in difference is to engage with oneself. This is where the work starts and, in reality, never ends.

5. This *is* a business or corporate issue. As such, it has to be addressed. Of course, there are realities and constraints governing this environment, but these shouldn't prevent a meaningful and authentic engagement with this all-important issue.

The benefits of harnessing diversity

The good news is that there are significant benefits to be had by an organisation's ability to harness diversity – important benefits that make the pain (and risk) of doing so well worth your while.

The three more important of these for organisations are:

1. Diversity enhances *innovation*. Innovation is critical to 'staying alive' in today's fast-paced and competitive world. Innovation is critical to ensuring that the services we offer are effective in pursuit of our organisational objectives. Innovation will be required, as criteria around how we are held accountable and measured might shift with changing circumstances and context.

   Of course, efficiencies are important: get this area wrong and you won't even be in the game! However, the need to consistently adjust and adapt to an exponentially changing world and market, one driven by forces we don't control, means that a vital survival skill is the ability to reinvent oneself and innovate. This innovation extends beyond mere product and service innovation; it extends to the ability to innovate one's entire business model. Diversity is an essential ingredient in the mix that makes this difficult work possible.

2. Diversity leads to *resilience*. Who amongst us, if asked whether we think that (put your organisation's name here) needs to be a 'resilient organisation' would shrug this attribute off as unimportant? In today's challenging environment, resilience is an essential characteristic. Harnessing diversity builds resilience. (*Note*: The longitudinal research conducted by psychologists Emmy Werner and Ruth Smith on resilience is well documented in their highly acclaimed book *Overcoming the Odds*, 1992, and in a companion volume, *Journeys from Childhood to Midlife: Risk, Resilience, and Recovery*, 2001.)

   Resilience can be defined as the 'ability to get back on your feet when knocked down' – and given this, it is something that becomes essential if we are to thrive in the ongoing and increasingly turbulent context that is our 'new normal'.

3. Diversity enables *authentic community*. Authenticity within organisations is becoming increasingly important. People have expectations concerning the 'smell of the place' – which is how Howard Schultz, CEO of Starbucks, describes organisational culture (*Onward: How Starbucks Fought for Its Life Without Losing Its Soul*, 2011). Diversity offers a tough road to authenticity, but it is a road that, if travelled, offers tangible rewards.

An important distinction: Variety vs. diversity

One problem is that we often confuse '*variety*' with '*diversity*'. This is an important and helpful distinction to make when discussing the merits of diversity and how to harness it within our organisations. In most organisations, when we talk about diversity we are really meaning variety.

The result is that we 'manage' diversity in such a way that we never realise the benefits nor understand true diversity. Professor Peter Hershock, director of the Asian Studies Program at the East-West Center in Hawaii, offers a brilliantly helpful analogy to understand the difference between variety and diversity (see *Valuing Diversity: Buddhist Reflection on Realizing a More Equitable Global Future*, 2012).

He contrasts a *zoo* with a *rainforest*.

In a zoo, one can see all the animals that one would hope to see in the wild, but here they are all confined to cages or enclosures. In a zoo, the 'system' is not self-sustaining and it would collapse if not managed or given external support – e.g., someone has to turn on the lights and feed the animals in order for the zoo to survive. This is variety. It is a quantitative index of simple multiplicity. It is a function of *co-existence*.

In a rainforest, there is both collaboration and competition. Different systems co-exist and evolve towards a state of balance and equilibrium. This is true diversity. It can be messy, chaotic, and is always adaptive. Diversity is a qualitative index of self-sustaining and difference-enriching patterns of mutual contribution to shared welfare. It connotes processes of meaningful differentiation. It is a function of complex coordination enriching *interdependence.*

Understanding this distinction helps us appreciate the extent to which organisational mindsets and behaviours will need to shift if we are to truly lead and 'manage' diversity in order to extract the benefits we have mentioned. In most cases within our organisations, a 'zoo mindset' (and structure) prevails. The challenge of unlocking and harnessing true diversity – of embracing more of a 'rainforest' mindset and culture – is not to be underestimated.

It is not simple, is it?

How then do leaders learn to lead diversity?

1. A crucial first step is to *identify your 'filters'* and the filters of your team members. As stated earlier, we all perceive and interpret the world through filters (or lenses). Identifying your filters and, more importantly, recognising their order or hierarchy (this can fluctuate depending on context) are important tools for enhancing self-awareness and developing empathy by understanding others from their point of view. Consciously or unconsciously, we default to our dominant filters to make sense of human behaviour. In a given situation, competing perspectives, explanations, and reactions are frequently grounded not in different filters, but in our personal filter hierarchies – in other words, the order in which we sift and prioritise information. By identifying these hierarchies, we can learn to recognise when dominant filters influence our personal behaviour (biases, triggers, and blind spots) and that of others, enabling a more informed and sophisticated leadership response. By highlighting difference, we discover ways to intentionally lead diversity. So we start to understand how we are different *from* each other, which then leads to the step #2…

2. The need to *value difference* or diversity. In other words, we choose to appreciate the fact that we are different from each other. There needs to be a sincere and heartfelt appreciation for the value of embracing diversity. If this is lacking then the challenges faced in meaningfully engaging diversity will overtake our best efforts. Don't assume that everyone will 'get this' and make sure that there is a real commitment to do this difficult work. Once we start to value diversity, it provides impetus to the third step…

3. The need to *intentionally engage* with diversity. It is not an accidental engagement, but rather an intentional mindset and actions that open up the possibilities that diversity offers. This is one reason why we love travel and getting to experience different places, people, and situations. Travel affords an experiential engagement with diversity like no other. A favourite quote is that of Mark Twain who wrote, 'Travel is fatal to prejudice, bigotry, and narrow-mindedness, and many of our people need it sorely on these accounts. Broad, wholesome, charitable views of men and things cannot be acquired by vegetating in one little corner of the earth all one's lifetime.' (*The Wit and Wisdom of Mark Twain: A Book of Quotations,* 1999).

The best and most practical way to engage is to make time to share and hear each other's personal story/journey. When we know each other's story, it opens up empathy and understanding that makes engaging in our differences easier and richer. Hearing each other's story is to venture into 'sacred territory' and needs to be treated with respect and skill. There are tools to enable effective storytelling exercises, and it is never a waste of time to build this into a team's agenda. For far too long, narrative (story) has been at the periphery of leadership development thinking and processes. It needs to be at the centre!

Smart leaders actively build diversity because they understand all this. Is it easy? No. Does it require a different mindset and skillset? Absolutely.

The challenge is to learn how to be different *for* each other by first recognising that we are different *from* each other. To be different *for* each other means that I am able to bring 'who I am' into the room in such a way that I add value to those there. Ultimately, we move from being different *'from'* each other to being different *'for'* each other so that we can be different *'together'*.

As a leader, this is the journey that is required; this is the journey on which you need to be able to say, 'we are embarked'; this is what it means to lead in today's world in order to thrive in tomorrow's world. This is the journey that is your journey.

There can be no more important task facing those in leadership. This matter goes to the very heart of what it means to lead people and invite their best in our collective business endeavours.

**Helpful questions for you and your team to consider
and discuss:**

- How are we (as individuals) different 'from' each other?
- What are my dominant biases or filters through which I see
  and interpret the world around me?
- How are these biases impacting on the work that we
  do together?
- What can we do to begin the journey of 'different *from*' to
  'different *for*'?
- How might we measure progress made along this journey?
- Are we (as an organisation) more like a zoo or a rainforest?
  What are the implications of this?
- What resources can we draw on to assist us in embracing and
  harnessing diversity?
- Do I know the (real) story of those in my team? How might
  we engage in a meaningful storytelling exercise as a team?
- When did I last have a meaningful conversation with someone
  who was very different to me?

Reflective Exercise: The Trusted Ten

One of our colleagues, Tamryn Batchellor-Adams, who is a psychologist, introduced us to a powerful exercise we recommend you do. It's one you can do with your team or individually.

Take a piece of paper and make six columns. Think of your inner circle – the people you really trust the most, those whose counsel you seek in making decisions or would trust with advice at work/personally. Write their names down in column 1. There can be a maximum of 10 people only – if you only have five or six names, then think about people you trust a lot but not quite your inner circle and add their names to the list until you have completed a list totalling 10 names. If you have more than 10 names, choose your top 10.

Once this is complete, give column 2 the heading *Gender*; column 3 the heading *Race/Ethnicity*; column 4 *Education Level*; column 5 *Age*; and column 6 *Nationality*. Now complete the particulars for each of the listed names you had in column 1 until all the names have their details filled out. For example, if the first name in column 1 was 'Ellen', work across row 1 filling in her specific details of gender, race, education level, age, and nationality. Do this for all nine remaining names.

Now look at your table. *What patterns do you notice?*

If you are male, are most of your trusted 10 also male? If you are female, are the majority of your trusted 10 female? Do your trusted 10 look similar to you in age or race or education level? Do the majority share your nationality? Chances are YES. We can change the top row of categories and replace them with language, sexual orientation, country of residence, religious views, anything really – the results generally come back with the same result: the trusted 10 are most often people very similar to you!

Why is this? Well, people tend to trust those who belong to the same types of in-groups as they do. If I'm religious, I'll tend to trust other people of my religion because I know I can draw on a set of common underlying values that mirror mine. It's the same for gender, age, etc. As we move our circle of trust wider to include people we are friends with but not extremely close to, the patterns may change. But our closest advisors and those we rely on most for sound insight are often an unconscious mirror of ourselves or those who share our values and background.

How is this problematic?

In the workplace, when leaders are given big projects or need to put together a team to think through strategy or deliver a project, they tend to draw automatically on those whom they trust the most within the organisation. Without knowing it, leaders unconsciously draw on certain prejudices that allow 'people like us' to be in their 'inner circle' at work. In doing so, they create a more uniform team that lacks real diversity and potential for different thought and insight. This becomes more problematic when we consider the current context of gender and race disparate C-suite positions that result in women or people of colour being 'single representatives' in top-level organisational teams.

Without leaders addressing their unconscious bias, everyone stands to lose – especially the organisation. This is because we not only sideline those who are different to us, thus perpetuating bias in the workplace, but we also severely limit the potential of teams by diluting their diversity.

If you want to establish robust and dynamic teams in your organisation, you have to start with addressing your own unconscious blind spots. Thereafter, as leaders, you can begin to actively put together teams of greater diversity. This means giving opportunities to people whom ordinarily you may have unconsciously overlooked, or perhaps even judged more harshly based on your personal bias.

11. Once Upon a Time: An Invitation to Rethink the Role and Importance of Story

'Humans think in stories rather than in facts, numbers, or equations, and the simpler the story, the better.' Yuval Noah Harari

'Instead of telling our valuable stories, we seek safety in abstractions, speaking to each other about our opinions, ideas, and beliefs rather than about our lives... academic culture blesses this practice by insisting that the more abstract our speech, the more likely we are to touch the universal truths that unite us. But what happens is exactly the reverse: as our discourse becomes more abstract, the less connected we feel. There is less sense of community among intellectuals than in the most "primitive" society of storytellers.' Parker Palmer

In this quote, Parker Palmer makes a bold and powerful assertion, one that we suspect the academics won't be too partial towards. But perhaps Palmer is correct. Human connection is regulated at the most fundamental level through story. It is our shared story that allows us to connect, to empathize and relate. Not to know another's story allows a distance that makes judging easier and prejudice more acceptable. It is the shared story that bridges the gap and creates the bond from which amazing things can be born. Stories matter a great deal, and this is something that is slowly starting to re-emerge in the literature and thinking orientated around leadership and organisations. We should not be surprised. In fact, that the role of story has been so reduced and frequently absent for so many decades should be the real surprise!

There are some important themes emerging in a converging world that smart leaders pay attention to, and one of these themes is the importance of story. There are two fundamental pillars underpinning why story is so essential in the theory and practice of leadership.

Firstly, we see the world not as it is but as we are. In other words, our lenses dictate how we see and interpret the world around us. This is why Daniel Goleman's framework of Emotional Intelligence (EQ) is so important and relevant.

Secondly, we lead out of who we are. Self-awareness is fundamental to how we see and how we lead, and these two are not mutually exclusive but rather are intertwined in a complexity that can only be made sense of through story. It is as we intentionally engage our own unfolding story that we begin to develop the self-awareness and intelligence that form the foundation of authentic leadership.

Simon Sinek explains in *Start with Why* (2011): 'We are drawn to leaders and organizations that are good at communicating what they believe. Their ability to make us feel like we belong, to make us feel special, safe, and not alone is part of what gives them the ability to inspire us.'

When we engage with our own stories and the stories of others, we find that we are able to see the world in new ways. In a remarkable TED Talk, Chimamanda Ngozi Adichie reminded us of the dangers of what she called 'a single story' (see http://bit.ly/AdichieTED). As a Nigerian studying in America, she was amazed at how little her fellow students knew of Nigeria and the world she came from. She was upset and offended by this. Yet, when she had an opportunity to visit Mexico, she was confronted by her own lack of knowledge and her own prejudices against Mexicans. She realised that it is our stories of the world – of each other – that create division between people, especially if we only have a single story of that world.

147

A powerful tool for connection

When we understand leadership as being about authentic connection, as being about influence rather than a title or position, then story becomes a powerful tool to understand and to use. We connect through our stories, and we live and are lived by our story. This is what makes storytelling so powerful and memorable, and yet we make little or no time for it within our organisations. We busy ourselves with data and concern ourselves with processes and efficiencies that we scrutinize, measure, and constantly analyse. Again, there is a place and appropriateness for all this, yet it comes at the neglect of what is really important – connection, both inside and outside our business.

The former masquerades as 'real work', and anything other than the activities that drive these things is seen to be an intrusion, a distraction, and sometimes a waste of resources – both time and effort. This is where we have missed it altogether. We have shied away from the very thing that ought to be central to our leadership – our story. We have built our muscles but neglected our souls. We talk earnestly of meaning and purpose in our work and in our workplace, yet we have forgotten the very building blocks that make this possible – our story.

So let us attempt to make what might sound like the ravings of a lunatic real for you in the challenge and daily practice of your own leadership. Leaders, after all, don't have time for this type of thing, right? Well, that is where you would be wrong. If you are too busy for the practice of story, then you are too busy and you are inadvertently diluting the very essence of your leadership influence.

Here then are three reasons to practice story and advice for how to go about doing so:

1. **Our organisational culture is framed by our stories.** The most important work for leaders is not that of strategic formulation and execution, but rather shaping and guiding organisational culture. It has been shown that the majority of strategic intent ends in failure, and the reason for this is not poor strategy – the main reason strategies fail is due to an organisational culture that is unable or unwilling to support the strategy (for more on this, see the excellent book *Results*, 2005, by Gary L. Neilson and Bruce A. Pasternack). A deeper exploration of culture will reveal the fundamental importance and role of story, and so as leaders go about building a healthy organisational culture, the place and role of story cannot be neglected. Of course, it often is, and that is why so much of our talk in the context of creating meaning and purpose in the workplace is hollow rhetoric met by cynicism and apathy.

So what can you do about it? Ask yourself (and others) how they see your organisation. What stories do they tell in answering such a question? (Ask them to tell you their experiences, not give you their analysis.) What stories are they not telling? What stories would you like them to tell? Could you describe your company's mission and vision free from the business jargon that usually accompanies such statements, and could you share what these are through telling some stories? Exploring such questions would be a good place to start, but it is a journey that will take you deeper into the heart of understanding the essence of culture within your organisation.

This understanding is not something that should be left or delegated to your human resources person/team; it is something with which you, as a leader, need to concern yourself. Asking for outside help might be useful; for example, Intel employed a cultural anthropologist to help guide them in this journey once they recognised its importance. And when we were working with a startup (now fully established and dominant) South African insurance company, Hollard, they were using a novelist and poet to help them frame and develop their company culture.

2. **Our connection one-on-one and group-to-group is determined by our revealed story.** We are living in what we describe as the 'Connection Economy' (see Chapter 3), meaning that our competitive edge is no longer only found in business efficiency, but rather in our ability to connect inside and outside our organisation. The 'war for talent', for example, is nothing other than a connectivity issue, and when leaders understand connection as fundamental to everything in their business, well then, things change. This understanding drives exceptional service, great employee engagement, and everything else – smart leaders know the importance of connection.

So what can you do about it? For one thing, re-examine those connection points for which you are responsible. The one-on-one encounters, the formal meetings, and the countless opportunities you have every single day to connect. Find your own 'coffee cup management' practice as championed by Brazilian businessman Ricardo Semler, and which he expounds on in his book *Maverick* (1995). Semler talks about the few minutes it takes to make and drink a cup of coffee, a practice that Brazilians are particular partial to, and using that drinking time to connect with someone in the office. He talks about the importance of standing at employees' workstations and using this time for initiating a more personal connection point.

He explains how easy this is by simply looking at photos or

kids' drawings on their desk and asking about these as a starting point. Building this practice into a habit realises powerful results and serves as a starting point to forge connection. Another option would be to rethink some of your orientation processes and developmental programmes (have storytelling sessions) and plan to drop in on some of these from time to time. 'Too busy for that', we hear you say… well then, perhaps you are too busy to be leading? Leadership is never about time… it is about how you use the time you have, and creating and fostering connection. That is the leader's responsibility.

3. **We remember stories, not PowerPoints.** Powerful communication is shaped by story. Smart leaders understand the importance of storytelling and see this as an art essential to effective messaging and communication. The use of story sits at the core of capturing both head and heart. Smart leaders live their story; they share their story – and that of their organisation; they actively look for story as a means of bringing the values of the organisation to life; they see story as an organising principle around which the core functions of the business operates. Yes, it is that important!

So, what can you do about it? Well, for one thing, next time you have a speech to give, try splicing in some stories. Not as jokes or as a sideshow, but find stories to illustrate the most important points you are trying to convey. It will exercise your imagination. You might need some practice, but wait for the results of such storytelling. We were once asked by a global company to assist them in forming and shaping their strategic process. We used a story framework/format to do the work with spectacular results, breathing new life into what is often a tired and mundane exercise. We know of breakaways that have been transformed through making time for storytelling, and there is almost no aspect of corporate life that cannot be impacted by an understanding of the use of story. Find ways to reframe data by way of story and become known as a storyteller yourself. In so doing, you will give permission for story to flourish within your organisation.

Citing G.K. Chesterton, author Neil Gaiman reminds us: 'Fairy tales are more than true – not because they tell us that dragons exist, but because they tell us that dragons can be beaten.' (*Caroline*, 2002)

If you are a leader, you ought to be a storyteller – in the richest sense of that word. This is not optional. Not if you're leading people, that is.

Reflective Exercise: Words Are Important

The way we talk about things, and the words we use to describe them, do make a difference and are important.

So, what words do you use to describe the people who work for you:
Subordinates?
Staff?
Employees?
'My people'?
Partners?

One of our clients, John Lewis, famously calls everyone who works for them 'partners'. You understand, of course, that it's not just a change of words we're after here; it's a change of mindset that is reflected in the words we use. But sometimes, you change the mindset by changing the words.

At another client, whilst delivering a high-level leadership development programme, we banned the use of the phrase 'the soft stuff'. We did this because the work our programme was doing was 'the soft stuff', but the way the phrase was used by senior executives was very negative and dismissive.

Words make a difference and are important.

What words might need to be changed in your organisation?

12. I, Robot: An Invitation to Say 'I Don't Know' in the Digital World

'The problem with quaint motivational quotations on Facebook is that you cannot always verify their authenticity.' Abraham Lincoln

You'll lose 100% of the shots you don't take.

You'll find this pithy advice in almost every motivational book. But being a cliché doesn't mean it isn't true. And here's another one: *You have to be in it to win it.*

In the business world, this maxim is applied when companies look seriously at new opportunities and take risks in new markets. This is the essence of business development, and most business leaders pride themselves in their ability to spot key growth opportunities and push their companies towards these. If we're living in a digital, connected age, then most of these opportunities will be linked one way or another to technology, and this is where we discover a big problem.

When it comes to technology, most leaders are seriously out of touch.

It seems strange to us how few CEOs are taking social media seriously. An American report released in early 2014 by Domo and CEO.com surveyed 500 top CEOs and discovered that less than 4% of them were active on Twitter. Fully two-thirds of them (68%) have no social media presence at all. The only network CEOs have a reasonable presence in is LinkedIn, but these are mainly just static profiles with no interaction or activity.

So, possibly the greatest revolution in communication is a mystery to the world's business leaders. This is a space they have no personal understanding of. So, how can they make decisions that are meaningful in this space? And how can they lead their companies into the digital age?

In the Domo and CEO.com report, a McKinsey research report is quoted as saying: 'By fully implementing social technologies, companies can potentially raise the output of employees by 20 to 25%. McKinsey's research also reveals that 72% of companies use social technologies in some way, but very few actually realise the full benefits.' Could it be because the implementations do not reach the very top? We are pretty certain this is key!

We do understand that social platforms like Twitter can be toxic and used in ways that many leaders feel are beneath them. Donald Trump has proven both the power and horror of Twitter in particular. We can understand that leaders looking on to the way President Trump has used Twitter might not see it as a model for their own usage, and they would be right. He is not. He is an aberration in the system.

What we do know is that the way people access information, make decisions, communicate, source news, air their own views, and choose products and services have all changed dramatically in the last decade. And all of these are now driven by social proof – which means that people go to social platforms for all of the above.

That doesn't mean that you or your organisation need to be obsessing about or spending huge amounts of time on social platforms. But it does mean that you must understand how these platforms work. It does mean you need to have systems that track what is being said about you and, in particular, what questions people are asking about, or to, you.

Of course, if we're talking about technology, let's not just obsess about the latest fad. We need to keep our eyes open to any and all technologies that might change the way our world, our industry, and our business works. It's something we have to keep on doing.

Even tech companies like Microsoft are not immune to falling behind the technology curve. Writing in *USA Today* in 2013, journalists Alistair Barr and Scott Martin suggested five things that Microsoft's new CEO, Satya Nadella, needed to do: embrace the Cloud, free its software from Windows, fix mobile, woo developers, and focus. These all seem pretty basic to us, but Microsoft was behind on all of them. As we write this in 2019, by the way, Satya has done this, and seems to be shifting the big tech giant remarkably well on tech issues.

Most companies should listen to the advice given to Satya – it is more widely applicable than might appear at first glance. Let's take a brief look at each one of these points and ask 'how' and 'if' it could apply to your own context.

1. **Embrace the Cloud**. Moving our data and software from the machines on our desks to remote drives in the ether, together with the integration this allows across multiple devices, is a game changer. The reality is that whereas 'the Cloud' was once considered unreliable and risky, such perceptions are fading quickly. What does the Cloud mean for your business and the way your people work?

2. **Free your software from Windows.** The broader point here is that you might need to 'free yourself' from restrictive systems, processes, and programmes that are simply no longer as effective or efficient as they once were. This usually proves to be much harder than it sounds – to 'free yourself', one has to overcome a mountain of obstacles, the sole purpose of which

are to maintain the status quo. This is what often keeps companies from being adaptive, nimble, and quick. Adaptive companies learn how and where to cannibalise themselves – how to destroy parts of themselves that might have been core DNA some time ago, but are now holding them back. It is a necessary part of how to 'stay alive' in an exponentially changing world. Ironic, isn't it?

3. **Fix mobile.** Mobile is the dominant route to information and quite possibly to your market. It certainly is already how younger generations connect, communicate, and source information. Failure to be asking the 'right questions' in this area, and what it means both inside and outside your business, might just mean you are left behind with only the dust of your competitors to keep you company. Putting mobile first needs to be a priority for your organisation.

But this means more than choosing a platform for your software – it requires an entire change to your development mindset. Consider the App Store or Google Play app on your phone (depending on what operating system you use) – every single day you check it, there are a number of apps that need updating. Many of the most-used apps on your phone are updated a few times each month. Is your company ready to upgrade and update your processes, systems, and 'user experiences' (of your staff, clients, customers, and suppliers) on a weekly or monthly basis?

4. **Woo developers.** In addition to actually needing developers for technology development, this advice is about who your best and core people are. So who would be your 'developers'? Make sure you know who the most important people to your business

success are and then ensure that your policies and service are geared towards making them happy. If your policies and processes don't make them happy, scrap them. The policies, not the unhappy people! They are not doing what they should be doing. The policies, not the people! Network, connect, go to – as opposed to waiting for others to come to you – and realise that what it takes to 'woo' these days has changed from what it once used to be. Dating skills have changed although some of the basic principles remain the same. You best know what has changed and what hasn't, otherwise you might just be home alone.

5. **Focus.** Never bad advice, ever. Focus, focus, focus. Know what you want, what you are good at, and what you need to do. Distraction is the enemy of achievement, and without focus the chances are you will never get to where you could have been – and that we term 'a waste'.

Given what we said above about leaders and social media, it's crucial we add to the list:

6. **Embrace social media.** If you, as a business leader, do not embrace social media, you are at risk of becoming a dinosaur in your industry and within your own company. Luckily, this is fairly easy to fix, but it will require you to step out into unknown areas where you have limited skills and no experience, where you risk making mistakes and possibly looking a bit foolish (none of this has to happen, of course, if you are prepared to get training and assistance – something most CEOs are not keen on). So, this boils down to a control issue really, and possibly a pride issue too, but the alternative is extinction.

Six steps to personally adapting to a digital age. How do you match up?

13. Experimentation: An Invitation to Rethink Failure

'Only those who dare to fail greatly can ever achieve greatly.' Robert F. Kennedy

'Even the great business visionaries and luminaries of our times often fail and have setbacks. Imperfection is a part of any creative process and of life, yet for some reason we live in a culture that has a paralyzing fear of failure, which prevents action and hardens a rigid perfectionism. It's the single most disempowering state of mind you can have if you'd like to be more creative, inventive, or entrepreneurial. The antidote is to try a small experiment, one where any potential loss is knowable and affordable. The revolution will be improvised.' Peter Sims, in *'Five of Steve Jobs's Biggest Mistakes'*, Harvard Business Review

'The only way to think like a leader is… to experiment with unfamiliar ways to get things done.' Herminia Ibarra

One of the smartest things you can do as a leader is to be curious about failure. Sounds like the entirely 'wrong' emphasis, doesn't it? But let us explain what we mean.

In business today there is a lot of talk about the need for innovation, and the subject of innovation is not unrelated to the broader topic of adaptability. In the global context, the need to adapt and innovate is self-evident. The problem, however, is that we have built organisations that often prize stability over adaptability; certainty over curiosity; measurement over creativity; performance over learning; efficiency over passion; and the short-term over the long-term.

Failure is an important part of the learning process. Without it, learning is diluted, usually too 'safe', and has little traction. Today, being a 'learning organisation' is simply not optional, and this means we must find 'better ways to fail' in that learning process. We tend to reward success, and of course there is nothing inherently wrong with recognising high performance. However, if the way we go about measuring and rewarding success reduces the willingness to experiment and learn through our failure, then there is a problem.

Failure is not something most leaders like talking about, and the word has been pushed into the shadows, becoming disconnected from the mainline leadership conversation. There are many things that have influenced why this is the case, including specific organisational cultures and the personality of the leader. Many leaders are what the Enneagram (a personality profiling tool) terms the 'need to succeed' type. For such types, failure is to be avoided at all costs. It is therefore not surprising that they would do little to encourage conversations around learning from failure and the role that failure can play in the bigger scheme of things.

We're not just talking about self-induced failures or things we tried and have not been successful at. We also have in mind those times when life did not go according to plan or when hardships came our way. We tend to try and bury these in the past. And yet to do so is to miss opportunities for growth and development.

A question we enjoy asking leaders is: *Where is the place of your deepest learning?* It is a profound and important question. The answer is usually one that speaks of deep loss or pain, of a circumstance or situation that is not one that the individual wishes to revisit. Somehow, though, this is what life serves to us and these are the conditions conducive to growth. Leaders need to be willing to host such conversations. You need to explore such territory on a personal level if you are to help others do it for themselves. Naturally, there is an appropriateness to all this and the need for a good sense of timing; but nonetheless, it is where the deeper leadership and learning agenda is to be found.

When it comes to failure, there would be a few things that as a leader you should keep in mind:

1. Failure is part of any journey; it is a necessary part of life.

2. In the pursuit of innovation, failure is guaranteed.

3. Being curious about failure will open the way to learn from failure.

4. Leaders fail. It is how you fail (and your response) that matters most.

5. Smart organisations understand that failure is necessary in adapting.

6. Adapting is non-negotiable in today's context.

Steve Jobs is a good example of a leader who understood the value of failure. Think about it: the Apple Lisa. The Newton. Macintosh TV. The Apple III. The Powermac g4 Cube. He delayed the introduction of the iPad and would have opposed the iPhone Plus size. Despite his brilliant understanding of how technology trends were developing, he messed up fairly regularly and spectacularly (although he got better with time – and practice).

In addition to product failures, Steve Jobs also made some really shocking business decisions – such as hiring John Sculley as his Apple CEO – the same John Sculley who instigated a 'coup' to overthrow him two years later. Or thinking that Pixar was going to be an excellent hardware company.

It's vogue these days to learn all sorts of lessons from Apple. Let's not forget to learn from their failures too. Our takeaway is that you shouldn't be scared of failure. And that if you have some big wins, people will soon forget your losses. And you're unlikely to have really big wins if you're not prepared to accept a few failures along the way.

Experiments are dangerous

There are dangers with workplace experiments, of course. The first danger is more obvious: some of them will fail. For some people, this is going to be personally dangerous for your career, especially if you work inside an organisation that has a low failure threshold. Ideally, the experiments you attempt should be as limited as possible to ensure that failure is not catastrophic or deeply damaging.

A more subtle danger though, for yourself and your organisation, is that you think you can appropriate other peoples' experiments and make them your own. In some cases, it is acceptable to be a good follower and to wait for others – braver, bolder, and with more resources than you – to try and fail and try again until they come across a clever formulae. However, especially when it comes to management techniques, it's not always appreciated that the culture that allows mistakes is often a prerequisite to the success of any experiments within that culture. Put more simply: you cannot simply copy the outputs or models another company comes up with and expect them to work in your company.

That's why at TomorrowToday Global we're thrilled to see that some organisations are already attempting to make adjustments today for the world they see coming tomorrow. They are future-proofing their organisations by being experimental. So we're excited when we discover companies and organisations still prepared to experiment.

Here are a few of our favourites from clients we work with or know:

Rotating the CEO

Chinese mobile phone company Huawei announced in 2013 that they would be rotating their CEO every six months in order to stay fresh. Three executives would share the CEO position. They explained: 'A rotating system for leaders is nothing new. In times when social changes were not so dramatic, emperors could reign for several decades and create periods of peace and prosperity.

'Such prosperous periods existed in the Tang, Song, Ming, and Qing dynasties. The rotational period for each emperor lasted several decades. Some companies in traditional industries rotated their CEOs every seven or eight years, and these CEOs experienced some prosperous times in their industries. Today, tides rise and surge; companies are springing up all over the place while others are quickly being swept away. Huawei hasn't found a way to adapt well to a rapidly changing society. Time will tell if the rotating CEO system is the right move or not.' Time will tell, indeed. This is an experiment worth doing.

Crowdsourcing: Inside and outside your organisation

Crowdsourcing is growing exponentially thanks to sites like Kickstarter and 99designs. Basically, crowdsourcing involves getting services, ideas, content, and/or funding by soliciting contributions from a large group of people. Many companies are experimenting with versions of both external and internal crowd-sourcing. At IBM, for example, 500 employees were given an allowance of $100 to pledge to different internal projects. There were 45 projects to choose from, and about half met their funding goal in order to be taken further within the company. Employees were able to ask questions and give input before they pledged, which gave them more buy-in. There also had to be enough volunteers per project for it to be considered viable and successful. The projects ranged from purchasing an office 3D printer to hosting a lecture series.

Meetings

Some of our clients are experimenting with meetings. There probably isn't a bigger time waster or efficiency killer than meetings, and yet hardly any attempts are made to experiment with different options. We've seen successful experiments involving standing only meetings, where no chairs are provided for participants. Other teams start meetings at strange times and run the meetings for unusual durations: 'Our meeting will start at 9:27 and run for 36 minutes.' Start exactly on time (everyone will be there, just to see if you are), and use a countdown timer in full view of everyone to keep to your allotted time. It sounds too simple, but unless you try it, you won't know if it could work for you, do you?

Communication: Death to email instead of death by email

If meetings are killers of efficiency, then emails are going to be the death of us completely. Most of us are buried under an avalanche of emails, yet too few companies are trying any experiments in changing email behaviour or even replacing email altogether. We've seen plenty of options that are worthy of trying, but you're going to have to experiment to find what works for you and your team. That is the point of this chapter, after all. Seriously, though, you need to be trying to replace email because we all know it's a system that is going to explode and hurt us all sometime soon.

Upwork, Fiverr, and other micro-outsourcing support services

It amazes us that audience after audience we ask about micro- and personal outsourcing just stare blankly. The concept is obvious, and if you think about it for a moment, you will realise that the concept is obvious and must exist. Websites that operate like eBay auction sites for skills abound around the web. Upwork is the big daddy, but there are some specialized sites too, like Fiverr.

Companies are now starting to use (or at least authorise the use of) these services. Some larger organisations, especially those requiring high levels of security, have created internal micro-outsourcing capabilities. The first company we came across to do this was Pfizer, which launched such a system (essentially an internal call centre and back office support hub) back in 2009. This is about outsourcing tasks (not jobs). It is genius, and can give your professional staff a few hours – or even days – free a month by getting someone else to do mundane work for them (we used to call this secretarial services – but micro-outsourcing is at an even higher level, and much cheaper).

If what we're saying here is unfamiliar to you, think of a task that you need to do that could be given to someone else at a digital distance. Go to Upwork.com and sign up for an account, then put in a request for someone to do this work for you. Or, if you need something artistic or creative designed, try using Fiverr.com instead. You'll discover it's easy, cheap, and effective. Go on. Try it.

A new approach to employee reviews: Just five words

Paul English, co-founder of Kayak.com, the travel search engine, fundamentally disrupted the process of giving employee reviews when he decided to make them all five – and only five! – words. Most HR professionals we know believe that reviews as we do them now are dead: they don't deliver the value they're supposed to. That's why Paul English's idea is not as crazy as it sounds. And we definitely think it's worth a try – at least with one of your company's stronger teams. As Paul explained in an interview in *Fast Company* magazine, each of the five words gets some explanation. But the focus is on five key things. Paul says he aims for a balance between positive and negative too. Here's an example of one he gave an employee recently:

1. FAST.

2. ATTENTIVE – People feel you listen to them, you're someone people like talking to because you completely focus on them.

3. UNTRUSTING – Although you try hard to understand people in your group, you don't completely trust people outside of your organisation that you can't control. And it creates a really bad dynamic when a manager likes people who work for him but doesn't trust people outside his group.

4. TOO CAUTIOUS – I said you're too cautious, and it sets the wrong vibe because our vibe is very much about forgiveness not permission. We want people to just ask. And if somebody feels like you're judging, it gives them pause.

5. TECHNICAL – Because you are in a very strong tech team and you are extremely technical.

Don't copy. Imitate!

These are just a few examples of workplace experiments other companies are trying. We have a long list of these, but it's better that we don't give you any more examples. Again, we remind you to be careful of simply copying other companies' experiments. Not everyone is going to benefit from Google's 20% discretionary time rule, for example (which Google are actually basically shutting down now anyway), or Ricardo Semler's 'Retire-a-Little' approach to taking leave, or any number of other experiments we could list. Part of what makes those successful is the entire ecosystem around such programmes, and not just the thing itself.

The examples we've used are mainly for inspirational purposes. Part of the benefit of workplace experiments is the very process itself that you and your teams will go through to devise and select the best experiments for your organisation and ecosystem.

Think about the following questions, for both yourself and your organisation:

1. What are you currently trying that has a fair chance of failure?

2. When was your last big failure? What did you learn from it?

3. Are you scared of failure?

Even having the conversation about experiments in the workplace is a good thing. So, go on, start a good thing today.

14. What If We've Got It Wrong: An Invitation to Rethink How We Develop Leaders

'Education is what survives when what has been learnt has been forgotten.' B.F. Skinner

'The mismatch between leadership development as it exists and what leaders actually need is enormous and widening.' Deborah Rowland

Some years ago, we asked a friend who was responsible for some of the most successful TV adverts in South Africa – she was the advertising agency's account manager for a fast food brand – what made the adverts so successful. 'That's easy,' she said, 'the client leaves me and my team alone to do what we do best – deliver on the brand and, in so doing, make award-winning adverts.' She went on to explain that the norm was for clients to constantly interfere with the creative design and process, thinking that they (the client) knew best when it came to what did or didn't work.

It doesn't make sense to pay an advertising agency a premium price only to then interfere with them doing their job. But that is what invariably happens. Of course, in most cases, as our friend explained, the advertising agency has to compromise on the creative and artistic integrity in order to keep the client happy.

For the most part, exactly the same thing happens in the design and execution of leadership development programmes. Leadership development programmes (LDPs) have become big business. A 2015 *Harvard Business Review* study estimated the annual amount spent on employee training and education at $356 billion.

Whilst it is hard to calculate exactly what part of that sizable budget goes into leadership development, the best guess is that it would be around $50 billion (annually). In many institutions responsible for leadership research and development, the 'cash cow' is their suite of inhouse and customised 'executive leadership' programmes. Inherent within these offerings is the need to 'keep the client happy' and thereby coming back for more. Metrics are designed accordingly, and these 'happy sheets' are given extraordinary attention as the barometer to how well things are going.

For several years we were part of an executive programme in China for a global company run by one of the world's top business schools. Built into the contract (between the client and the business school) was a condition that should the participants' ratings of the programme drop beneath a certain point, the business school would incur a financial penalty. In addition to this, the inhouse bonuses for those involved in the co-design (together with the business school) would also be impacted by bad participant ratings. As the ratings dipped close to the critical number (for a variety of reasons not related to the actual content and value of the programme), the behaviour and efforts of the personnel from both the business school and the company became increasingly feverish and chaotic. The focus shifted to keeping delegates happy rather than on learning, value, or the programme integrity. The learning agenda became a battleground as desperate attempts were made to 'save the programme', and some of what played out was almost comic, were it not so tragic.

So, how did it get to this – a scenario that sadly is not uncommon?

The business school makes promises to the client that it cannot keep and becomes 'risk adverse' in the learning process. The HR and L&D gatekeepers in the company become too prescriptive and hands-on, not trusting the very LDP experts they have employed. The tail wags the dog, and the disruption so necessary for learning is removed from the programme. It is that simple and that complex. It is the great irony: the message (from the business school) for the client to be willing to change their business models and challenge their assumptions and orthodoxies is a message that goes unheeded by the messenger!

If you go to the 'experts'... then trust them!

Companies want to develop their leaders, and often feel that they need external assistance to do so. They choose partners to help them, but then won't let these partners do what needs to be done to actually develop their leaders effectively. Clients interfere, intervene, override, and prohibit activities and approaches that the external experts would prefer to use. This leads to risk-reducing behaviour from the selected partners, and so a vicious cycle begins that leads to boring, ineffective, paint-by-number LDPs.

The generic, risk-reducing approach adopted by many business schools is leaving many clients dissatisfied with the return on the considerable investment made in such programmes. Whilst good content is being shared, very often it doesn't translate into tangible benefits in the workplace. In short, behaviours aren't changing. It must be said that this isn't always the fault of the business school as often not enough effort is made in bridging the programme to the work reality of the participants.

There are significant cracks appearing in the current model of leadership development and a growing dissatisfaction with, and questioning of, the current model. However, the investment in this current model makes it difficult for those engaged in this dance not only to challenge it, but to find better and more relevant alternatives. Barbara Kellerman's book *Professionalizing Leadership* (2018) provides a remarkable (and scathing) insight and assessment on the state and condition of the 'leadership industry'.

Whether done internally or through business schools, there will be five specific factors leading to the demise of the current models of leadership development:

1. The realisation that the return on investment is not adding up.
2. The unwillingness of the next generation of leaders to invest in the current model.
3. The shift in how learning takes place, fuelled by a new breed of learners emerging with different needs and expectations.
4. The rise of MOOCs (massive open online courses) that allow any individual anywhere to access some of the world's top courses and content, often for free and almost always in a more convenient way than formal workplace-based training.
5. The fact that it is patently obvious that hours and days invested in leadership programmes are not producing the kinds of leaders companies need.

The top three fault lines running through current leadership development programmes are:

1. **They are seen as programmes and not a process**. This induces the wrong kind of measures and emphasis. The biggest pitfall of this distinction is that the 'programme' serves in isolation from the meaningful integration of learning in the workplace. In some cases, what is learnt on the programme actually gets in the way of effectiveness in the workplace. The responsibility for this fault line rests as much with the client as it does with the educational institute tasked with the design.

2. **The wrong things are measured at the wrong time.** Daily

measures that track satisfaction drive most programmes, where any score below 4.5 (out of 5) is not acceptable. What this means is that anytime a low score is received, everyone goes into a tailspin. But what if measuring progress or learning cannot (always) be linked to fun, enjoyment, and delegate satisfaction in the moment? What happens if we need people to feel decidedly uncomfortable in order to advance their learnings? What if the real measure of learning can only be done months after the actual event? We need a serious rethink of what is measured, how we do this, and even why we do it.

3. **Too much emphasis is placed on keeping the client happy.** We call this the 'Goldilocks Principle' – too hot, too cold, too soft, too hard, too little, too much, and so it goes. The end result is a compromise in which everyone continues to smile and the game goes on: leadership processes that fail to grow leaders. What is to be done about it? How do we stop the music and start a new dance – one that is relevant, needed, and that will be effective? When the client approaches the 'expert' or educational institution, the client needs to trust the educators and allow them to do their job. What tends to happen instead is that the company constantly interferes with the architecture and design of the process, resulting in appeasement – a lot of activity but little change. The biggest outcome of all this is 'safe' programmes designed to keep the participants happy and comfortable. It seems the higher up the organisational tree the programme is aimed, the greater the spin to keep it safe and comfortable.

Five simple but important 'design' questions

The approach to designing leadership development programmes needs to change and focus on five important design questions:

1. Who is the **learner**?
2. What **is it** they need to learn?
3. How (best) will they **learn it**?
4. How (best) can it then be **taught**?
5. How will we **know** that learning has occurred?

They are basic questions. The failure to acknowledge or see the change that is occurring, or required, in each of these areas is what is causing many current programmes to fall short of what they could or should be.

Important areas underpinning leadership development efforts are under severe pressure to adapt to a changing world.

Content has never been easier to get, is often free, and is now the easy part of the equation. This hasn't always been the case as we have prized subject experts who guard their knowledge, and without whom learning cannot take place. All this is shifting. Those guarding their knowledge (as do many business school academics) are fast becoming increasingly isolated and irrelevant in their ability to meaningfully influence and engage the bigger picture.

The prevailing *methodology* has been 'teacher-tell', and the classroom has been the epicentre for our learning process. We know that this is seldom the most effective way to learn but are often afraid to try other means – our metrics haven't been designed to cope with such alternatives. It is easier to trust in a programme rather than a process; it is easier to lecture than to experience; and it is safer to have a schedule and curriculum to control, rather than understand the importance that experimentation and disequilibrium play for authentic learning to take place. The latest fad is for LDPs to move towards 'experiential learning'. This takes the form of carefully controlled and highly sanitised 'site visits' and/or 'classroom activities' – itself an oxymoron given the static design and restrictive nature of the classroom!

The *platform* is perhaps where the biggest shift is taking place. The move to social business and technology-driven platforms is where the biggest discord sits. Older leadership architects feel 'lost' in this space whilst a younger, technically capable crowd is emerging who expect to find technology and social platforms built into their learning experience. Add to this competing online offerings, and it's clear that the old approach is dying a quick and brutal death. In 2017, TomorrowToday Global invested considerable time and resources in developing our online Future of Work Academy. It is both practical and cost-effective in helping ensure that the user develops the necessary skillsets for thriving in tomorrow's world. A feature of the design is the possibility to white label the entire offering, allowing companies/ business schools to use it 'as their own'. There has been worldwide uptake from individuals and companies alike, yet little traction with business schools.

Why is this?

Those we thought would be most excited by this offering have shown the least appetite for a tool that could add meaning to their rhetoric of providing 'sustainable learning' to underpin their programmes. In part, it is due to a malaise and political inertia that are hidden within many of these institutions. When the teachers fail to be learners, the end is in sight!

Change in this space is inevitable. Smart companies are asking different questions when it comes to ensuring that their leaders are competent to lead into the future. We need to be willing to challenge much of the current paradigm and prevailing wisdom when it comes to how best to do this. Our current models are tired, and rethinking leadership development is critical to ensure that our organisations will adapt to a complex and changing world.

Becoming a learning organisation – from the top down

Here is a suggestion for you if you really want to go beyond mere lip service: insist that every member of your executive team be present at (and you select an amount/time here) specific leadership development programmes. Imagine the impact of senior people showing up to learn, build relationships, and hear firsthand what is being taught and learnt by the leaders throughout your organisation. We know this would reverberate throughout the organisation, for we have often asked course participants (your people) what they would make of such behaviour. You should hear their answers… well, you could if you were there!

Here would be another suggestion closer to home: open-ended questions that lead to open-ended discussions. In other words, an intentional learning agenda, rather than one of operational matters perhaps thinly disguised as 'strategy'.

How are you learning from the future and what is it you are reading? Many leaders will dismiss all this with 'we don't have time for that'. Yet if you continue like that for long enough, you will soon have plenty of time on your hands as there will be no business to lead!

If yours is not a learning organisation, it will not survive the future. The way current leadership developments are conducted does not necessarily mean that learning is taking place. Something needs to change, and all those involved in the process that is leadership development have a voice and role to play in the changes that are needed.

Leadership also needs to recognise that real learning happens at the edge of comfort. Real learning is invariably found in the zone of discomfort, and we know this to be true when we look at life itself.

Too many leadership development programmes play it too safe, and the air-conditioned, five-star comforts have reduced learning to listening to talking heads, punctuated by sorties to decimate the considerable buffet tables that lie in wait outside the room. There is a lot of information being transferred, but little real, game-changing learning taking place.

The measure of this is how little leadership behaviour changes once the programme is over. Has the status quo been maintained, or is the company moving forward?

Developing future leaders is too important a task to be undercut. Something needs to be said and the status quo needs to be challenged.

A final word on this subject

If you find yourself in any way involved or interested in developing leaders and the direction this needs to take for tomorrow's world, you need to read Kellerman's book (*Professionalizing Leadership*). On pages 174/5, she offers a list of 20 features that ought to characterise leadership development programmes. As a matter of curiosity, we measured the best LDP (in our opinion) that we are involved in, and it was able to tick off at least 18 (arguably 19) of the 20 features! Sadly, many of the other business school LDPs we are part of score 5 or less. No wonder the clients are unhappy with the long-term benefits (or lack thereof) they are seeing.

We need to, as a matter of urgency, rethink how we teach how to lead. Our tomorrow depends on it.

New Pictures of Our Leaders

Picture a leader. Seriously, get a mental picture of a leader in your mind now.

These pictures of leaders are important. Just compare the mental image of a rugged individual in military uniform standing on top of a mountain peak staring at the horizon to an old woman kneeling in a squatter camp, hand-feeding a child dying of starvation. Both Napoleon Bonaparte and Mother Teresa led influential organisations that changed the world. But they couldn't be more different as people. And the skills required by each of them to be a leader in their contexts were very different too.

Where are you finding pictures of leadership? These pictures become models and then shape our expectations. Is your picture that of the commander-in-chief, the captain of the ship, the sports coach, the pilot of the plane, the judge of the court, the president of the country, the dictator of the nation, the head of the volunteer charity, the conductor of the orchestra, the director of the movie, the parent, the priest, the politician, the professor?

- Which of your pictures of leadership are most invitational?
- Which pictures of leadership have dominated your organisation's history?
- Which of these pictures of leadership are your leadership development programmes most likely to produce?
- What are the implications, for your organisation, of this model of leadership?
- Which do you think might be outdated in your current context?
- Where can you go to find new pictures of leadership?
- What picture do *you* give off as a leader?

15. Maintaining Balance When Shift Happens

'Everyone thinks of changing the world, but no one thinks of changing himself.' Leo Tolstoy

In April 2012, captivating pictures of Licia Ronzulli and her seven-week-old daughter, Victoria, went viral on social media. Why? It was taken in a voting session at the European Parliament in Strasbourg where Licia was a MEP from Italy, and every so often she would lean forward to kiss her child. The voting session was on proposals that were before the Parliament to improve women's employment rights. It was not one of those 'bring your child to work' days, and although Licia admitted to being partially motivated by the attention it would draw to her cause, it is a practice she has since maintained.

The mother-daughter images sparked a lot of debate about the role of women at work, parenting, gender equality, and other such topics. Licia was as praised as she was criticised. There was very little 'middle ground' surrounding the issues framed by the photos.

What we would like to focus on is not so much the 'right – wrong' of Licia's decision, but rather on how this single image powerfully captures a societal shift. That shift has continued to gain momentum in the decade since it happened, and now we're in an era of #MeToo and feminist activism. Around the world, women are gaining rights they haven't had before (in 2018, women in Saudi Arabia finally were allowed to drive cars), are being elected into leadership positions they haven't had before (the Democratic Party in the USA brought more women and minorities to Washington in the 2018 mid-term elections than ever before), and women are proving themselves in times of extreme stress (such as Prime Minister of New Zealand Jacinda Ardern's steely response to the tragic mass shooting in Christchurch in 2019). It has been a century – and much more – in the making, but like many exponential changes we've talked about through this book, the role of women in society is now experiencing faster change than ever before (even as some people believe it isn't changing fast enough). This is just one example of many that prove one main point: our world is changing, at a deep values level.

Dealing productively with shifting values is not easy. It is not easy for individuals, nor is it easy for society at large. It also poses one of the biggest leadership challenges as leaders find themselves consistently required to lead their people through change (and as we've just talked about, experiments too) within their organisations. When values shift, it always leaves hordes of people behind, and they are easily recognisable if you listen to the language they use. It is punctuated by the past tense, and it seems that they are walking forwards yet with their heads turned backwards. Their view is locked more into the rear-view mirror than it is looking down the road.

This work can be exceedingly draining for leaders. And it has the potential to be damaging too.

The dangers of being a leader

In their book *Leadership on the Line* (2002), Ron Heifetz and Marty Linsky warn leaders of the dangers of being the leader. Especially in changing times, leaders often find themselves in the crosshairs, targets of those who wish to cling to the status quo, or opponents who have different visions for change. Amongst the great advice offered in their book, the following points stand out for us:

1. **Get on the balcony** – we have mentioned this before, but it is worth repeating. Great leaders today understand the necessity of getting a big picture view of their organisations. In this case, it is to see patterns, minimise one's own emotional responses, and react (or not!) in ways that will help the community engage in the adaptive challenge that it faces.

2. **Think politically** – relating to people in ways that lead them through adaptive change. This requires developing allies, keeping the opposition (those most negatively affected by change) close, gaining trust with those who are uncommitted to the change, and thinking ahead when implementing plans – specifically considering the implications for other people and how they might respond. Smart leaders find partners, including authority figures and members of the factions for whom change will be very difficult. Keep these 'opponents' close and acknowledge their loss. Point out the values in the organisation that support the change and the reasons it is needed, but also acknowledge and name the loss that will be suffered by members of the community. You may also need to accept casualties in a change process.

3. **Orchestrate the conflict** – cultivate an environment where passionate disagreement is permissible whilst keeping control of the temperature, remembering that the job of the adaptive leader is to orchestrate the conflict, not become it. Leaders of adaptive change must manage the pace and process of change to ensure that the stress such change generates does not destroy the organisation, or cause factions within it to heighten their efforts to 'take out' the leader.

4. **Give the work back** – you 'stay alive' in leadership by reducing the extent to which you become the target of people's

frustrations. Smart leaders think constantly about intervening only in timely and responsible ways, and allowing the right people to take responsibility. Heifetz and Linsky point out that 'by trying to solve adaptive problems for others, at best you will reconfigure it as a technical problem and create some short-term relief.'

5. **Hold steady** – in the midst of the pressure and heat that comes with the implementation of adaptive change, leaders need to hold their poise by taking the heat, letting the issues develop naturally, and keeping a focus on the issues. The community must sense the urgency of the challenge. That means they cannot be distracted by other, more compelling crises. They must understand how deeply it affects them, must sense that they can master any required learning, and must get the right signals from authority figures. Leaders in adaptive challenges must be prepared to receive angry, attacking actions from members of the community without reacting defensively. These can be especially hard to take when they come from friends or allies.

6. **Hold onto others** – the best way to keep your balance is to support others and be supported by them. Different people experience shifts differently. For some, the shift that you are experiencing represents their stability. Be aware of this and don't assume 'your normal' is 'everyone else's normal'. Challenge assumptions and look for the opportunity of new support rather than bemoan the loss of old supports.

Heifetz and Linsky also have some excellent advice for leaders who need to hold steady:

- **Manage your hungers** – of power and control, affirmation and importance, and intimacy and delight.

- **Anchor yourself** – by distinguishing the role from your own self, keeping confidants but not confusing them with allies, and seeking sanctuaries.

- **What's on the line** – asking the question: Why lead? And remember always that leadership is a labour of love for others.

- **Sacred heart** – keeping an innocent, curious, and compassionate heart through the hurts and scars of leading by finding ways to refresh your body and spirit.

The leadership ethic

Tom Peters once said, 'The problem is not that they are not watching what you do, the problem is they are.' He is right. Leaders are under greater scrutiny than they have ever been due to the available technology and the context of a connected world. Of course, leaders have always been under scrutiny. It is just that it is now unrelenting, unforgiving, and news, both good and bad, travels fast. Leaders find themselves in a goldfish bowl, not always of their own making.

Almost daily one reads of prominent leaders who are exposed in some or another way by the media. Shocking details of often sordid or corrupt private lives are making headlines, and revealing character flaws out of keeping with the leadership positions and responsibilities they hold. We wonder just how they could have maintained such duplicity and how they thought they could get away with it!

What often masquerades as leadership is nothing of the sort. Authentic leadership is about the character ethic. You lead out of who you are, and today leadership has been confused with positional power.

Just because you hold a leadership position does not make you a leader. In fact, leadership is perhaps one of the most abused terms and concepts in today's world. It is a world in which leadership is often proclaimed prematurely, and credit given where judgment should be reserved. It is a world that confuses leadership with celebrity or activity.

Perhaps the test of authentic leadership is to simply pose a basic question: Is anyone following? If no one is following, there is no leadership.

Where influence is exerted, leadership is being practised. Putting aside deeper debate around the 'good' and 'bad' when understanding leadership as influence, the point is that leaders have both followers and exert influence. When the best of authentic leadership is practised, it evokes engagement rather than compliance. But it might also provoke a backlash, and you need to be ready for that too.

Protect yourself.

16. Doing and Being – and What to Do Next

'Jazz comes from who you are, where you've been, what you've done. If you don't live it, it won't come out your horn.' Charlie Parker

Charlie Parker was a genius when it came to the saxophone, and his quote is spot-on, both for jazz and when it comes to leadership – *especially* when it comes to leadership.

Leadership is about who you are. It's about character. It's about looking inwards in order to lead outwards. The source of leadership is within rather than a set of external skills. The best leaders are those who know themselves, know their strengths, and play to those strengths. They understand something of the connected, relational, and paradoxical nature of the world in which they live and lead. They embrace change as an opportunity rather than a threat, and they remain humble, lifelong learners who find wisdom in the small, the simple, and the overlooked.

Of course, the requirements for leaders today are changing as the world changes. Kevin Kelly, executive editor of *Wired* magazine and member of the Global Business Network, writes in *The Inevitable: Understanding the 12 Technological Forces That Will Shape Our Future* (2017) that, 'The network economy is reshaping and revolutionizing every sector of business.' In this Connection Economy, relationship forms the core organizing principle. It represents a fundamental shift in the way we think about the world and in how we understand leadership. Today leaders need to be agile, nimble, and adaptive. The real challenge is turning these adjectives into behaviours that can be seen and perhaps measured. Leadership needs constant work. To assume otherwise is a danger to both oneself and those being led.

Smart leaders will also be those who are able to create and build process and relationship into the very DNA of their company. They will change what they pay attention to in the organisation. They will focus on things more fundamental to strong relationships and will be attentive to the workplace's capacity for healthy relationships, in addition to its organisational form in terms of tasks, functions, span of control, and hierarchies. Smart leaders will need to become savvy about how to foster relationships and participate in networks as a means of nurturing growth and development.

Six enemies of adaptability – and what to do about them

Models of evolution show us that it is not the most intellectual of the species that survives, and it is not the strongest that survives; rather, the species that survives is the one that is able best to adapt and adjust to the changing environment in which it finds itself. It is not the strongest or the most intelligent that will survive, but those that can best manage change.

Given the critical need to be adaptable and the urgency to ensure adaptive intelligence at both a personal and organisational level, it makes sense to identify what might stand in our way – what might be the enemies of adaptability.

Here would be six common 'enemies' that thwart adaptability, and some tactical questions/suggestions as to how to defeat them.

1. Knowing for certain

'It is not what you don't know that gets you into trouble. It's what you know for sure that just ain't so', wrote Mark Twain (see *The Wit and Wisdom of Mark Twain: A Book of Quotations*, 1999).

A 'knowing for certain' leads to fixed assumptions. Fixed assumptions lead to an arthritic condition that limits flexibility. When we know 'for certain', it means that we stop asking questions or that we develop huge blind spots that allow bad habits to breed unchecked. Curiosity and questions are important in galvanising adaptability, and when there is an absence of curiosity and questioning – or, worse still, when they are actively discouraged – the casualty is adaptability.

Reflective Questions/Action:

- *What is it you 'know for certain that just ain't so'?*
- *Add this question to your next team agenda and see what your team comes up with.*
- *What are the questions you should be asking, but aren't? Why not?*

2. Habits

Being adaptable requires identifying mindsets and behaviours that we need to change. Of course, 'wanting' to make this change is an important part of the equation! Habits can get in the way of such change. It is hard to change old habits and develop new ones, but this is exactly what adaptability demands. Identifying the habits that are blocking a change in both mindset and behaviours is the first step in gaining a clear picture of what needs to be done in order to start the adaptive process. Flexible mindsets and behaviours are an essential part of what it means to be adaptive.

Reflective Questions/Action:

- *What are some of your 'work habits' (the way in which you approach your job)?*

- *Where did they come from and are they still serving a future-fit purpose?*
- *Which of these might need to change as you think about the work you will be doing three years from now?*

3. Fear

Fear is a very real block to developing adaptive intelligence. For some this will be more of an obstacle than it will be for others. The fear blocking adaptability will have many guises: What if I fail? What will I lose? What will I have to let go of? What will others say or think?

And so the questions will keep coming. Fear can lead to a very real paralysis that inhibits or blocks adaptability. Identifying this fear and facing it (easier said than done) is the start in overcoming it and embracing adaptability.

Reflective Questions/Action:

- *When you think of the future – what do your fear the most? Why?*
- *What might be your 'sense of loss' in making any of the changes that you feel will need to be made if you are to adapt?*

4. Organisational hierarchy

A hierarchical structure makes adaptation far more problematic. The reason is that affecting change can only really start from the top in a hierarchy. The lower levels (often acutely aware of the need to change and adapt) are usually powerless to affect the necessary change. The 'command-and-control' leadership style that usually is indicative of a hierarchy means that others within the structure are unable to initiate change. Information and control flow 'downwards'. Over time this contributes to the development of an unwillingness (deliberate or not) to initiate within the 'lower levels', and a kind of 'wait to be told' type of malaise sets in.

Research reveals that creating opportunities for self-organisation is a characteristic of adaptive intelligence and creating such opportunities results in increased sustainability. This should be all the motivation needed for leaders to ensure that they work hard to create such opportunities within their structures!

Reflective Questions/Action:

- *How might your structure be inhibiting the development of adaptive intelligence within your organisation?*
- *How could you increase opportunities for your team/ organisation to 'self-organise'? (Why not discuss this with them?)*

5. Short-term thinking

Short-term thinking means that the changes we make tend to be incremental and the action taken is in response to immediate pressures or opportunities. Many of the metrics in place drive and reinforce a short-term thinking mentality within business, and this is extremely dangerous. Leaders need to lift their heads and ensure that they and their team are 'looking out the window'. They need to be looking at the horizon and — as we in TomorrowToday like to call it – 'thinking like a futurist'. Smart leaders intentionally cultivate questions and conversations that force their team to consider the long-term consequences to the decisions and actions taken today. The issues around climate change have helped raise the awareness and importance of thinking long-term.

Reflective Questions/Action:

- *How far into the future are you and your team thinking?*
- *What are you measuring (and why)? How might this impact on your ability to think long-term?*

6. Spending too much time on the dance-floor

In the adaptive leadership model, a distinction is made between the 'dance-floor' and the 'balcony'. The idea is that leaders need to spend more time on the balcony, from where they are able to get a different perspective of the dance-floor. When on the dance-floor, one's perspective is limited to the immediate surroundings, and in a world that is complex, connected, and fast changing, being on the dance-floor can be dangerous because of what is unseen. Most leaders spend too much time on the dance-floor. A quick and easy 'test' of this would be to look at your last few leadership team agendas. The chances are that you will see an agenda dominated by 'operational issues' (the dance-floor) and little that is forcing the conversation to consider the bigger picture, the 'out-there' disruptions that need to be given careful attention.

Spending too much time on the dance-floor inhibits the ability to see the adaption that is needed. It feeds off of 'short-term thinking' and means that dance moves are honed rather than calling for an entirely new dance.

Reflective Questions/Action:

- *Review your last few agendas and put the dance-floor/balcony assumption to the test.*

- *What could your individual/collective balcony look like? How could you begin to access it, and how will you create accountability to such?*

These six 'enemies of adaptability' represent but a start in what might be your most important journey as a person and/or as a leader. Intentionally building the capacity to be 'future fit' – or to adapt to a changing context in order to thrive – cannot be emphasised enough. This is important work at both a personal and at a leadership level.

Shifting the dial as a leader

In the Connection Economy, the competitive edge is not situated in business efficiencies, but rather is found in the quality of the connections – both external and internal. The so-called 'war for talent' is a prime example of this shift in where competitive advantage is to be found. Business efficiency is important but it is now taken as a given – if you are not efficient, you are simply not in the game. To help you join the game, here are some different categories to consider when plotting your company's future and considering its next move.

1. **On 'talent':** Ask if your current strategy and HR plan are really working. Don't ask those who designed it. Go and ask those for whom the plan has been put in place – those you consider 'talent'. You might just be surprised by what you hear.

2. **On relationships:** In the new economy, relationships will ultimately be more important than transactions. In other words, you'll need a fundamental understanding that in this Connection Economy, relationship transcends transaction. Whilst efficient, cost-effective transactions remain important business practices, more will be required in tomorrow's world. The customer will demand relationship, and that is what will determine loyalty and create word-of-mouth sales. How does your organisation go about developing relationships, and how healthy are they?

3. **On your work-life balance:** As a leader you probably don't have a 'work-life' balance! But you should have a balance, and the fact that you don't means that your direct reports don't either. It is a dangerous and unsustainable situation. Think about what you can do to re-establish some sort of work-life equilibrium and then do it. Better still, ask your partner (and kids) what they think you could do to establish that balance – and listen!

4. **On strategy:** The old models simply don't translate in the fast, connected, complex, and different world that now shapes our reality. It is not that they were bad models – they were excellent for... well, 'the past'. Newer models are emerging, and if you wish to see a glimpse of the future thinking when it comes to strategy, then read William Duggan's *Strategic Intuition* (2007).

5. **On intentionality:** Embedded within the invitational leadership model is the notion of intentionality. Smart leaders act with intentionality – they know *why* they are doing something, if not always certain about *how* they need to be doing it. Intentionality means that when things work, you know why they work; and importantly, when things don't work, you know why they didn't work.

6. **On leadership:** If you are not a 'learner leader', you are not fit to lead into the future. Being 'future fit' as a leader will require you to be prepared to learn, unlearn, and relearn. Experience has never counted for as little as it does today when facing the exponentially changing and uncertain future. If that is all you are bringing to the party (your experience), you are in trouble (as is your organisation). Write down something you feel you need to learn, unlearn, and relearn... do it now.

7. **On personal resilience:** You will need it to survive the future, but you know that already. Personal resilience depends (amongst other things) on having a hopeful picture of the future – something to live towards. What is this for you? If you can't immediately articulate what it is, the chances are that you don't have a compelling personal vision of hope for your future – the absence of which erodes your resilience.

8. **On organisational resilience:** This depends on three things: firstly, the opportunity to participate; secondly, caring relationships; and, thirdly, high expectations. How does your company rate in these three areas? If you are not certain, then you may or may not be developing the DNA for resilience. Better to know that you are building resilience than hoping you are doing it.

9. **On social media:** There are two things you need to know about social media: firstly, it is not optional, and secondly, it is a mind shift before it is a technology 'buy'. Road test the adoption of social media in a select and contained area of your business before applying it to the broader spectrum. If you are clueless in this area, then do some reverse mentoring. Find a 'bright young thing' in your company and ask him or her to teach you how to 'connect the dots' in the world of social media. It will send out a powerful message – and don't believe that you can't teach an old dog new tricks.

10. **On listening:** Listen to customers, staff, suppliers, others... really listen! The individual now has unprecedented power to 'create noise'. If you don't listen or take feedback seriously, you might just find yourself dealing with a social media storm that is virtually impossible to control. Given how the rules of the game have changed when it comes to the broadcasting of information and opinion, how we listen also needs to change. You cannot let your listening skills lag behind your other efficiencies and competencies. Address any imbalance immediately, especially given the influence and impact of social media in today's context.

11. **On feedback:** Ensure that reliable feedback (of course, this is another way of saying really listen) is not only gathered but is acted on or synthesised. All growth, be that in the biological world or that of organisations, occurs through what has been described as the 'feedback loop': Action – Feedback – Synthesis. Without feedback there can be no growth – assuming, of course, it is incorporated into new actions. What systems do you as a leader have in place whereby you can benefit from reliable feedback? The tragedy is that many leaders have either intentionally or unintentionally placed themselves *above* direct feedback on their own performance. Yes, there is a close focus on delivery when it comes to the bottom line, but beyond that focus there is little else. Sometimes this means that delivery comes at a high price – one that goes unnoticed until it is too late.

12. **On leadership development programmes (LDPs):** If you are leading a large organisation, the chances are you spend a great deal on LDPs. The thinking is good but often the practice isn't. Look at how you measure the success of these programmes – your ROI. Most current measures focus on the wrong things and little, if anything, really changes. Authentic learning requires disruption, discomfort, and challenge. Most current LDP models 'play it too safe' to facilitate real and sustained learning. If you are going to invite a business school or outsourced partner to deliver your LDP, then let them get on and do it. Too many L&D people (in your organisation) meddle in the design process and confuse the outcomes. Tell the service provider what it is you are looking for, how you would ultimately like to measure it, and then have them design something wild. Have the courage to let them do the real work needed. Evaluate after six or twelve months, not at the end of each module. If you don't believe me that your L&D people are

interfering, then go and talk to your service provider (off the record, of course) and get the real story. It may surprise you, assuming the service provider is bold enough to be honest!

13. **On reading:** Too busy to read? Then you are too busy. Select carefully what you read and get your people reading as a way to infuse learning and thinking throughout your team/company. Start a book club and leverage the insights and learning that emerge. It is easier than it may sound and will cost little, other than some time.

14. **On your balcony:** Is your team both familiar with and comfortable with 'being on the balcony'? We have seen why it is important to get off the dance-floor and be on the balcony if we are to see the disruptive changes that will impact our business and/or industry. A context of disruptive change necessitates a 'balcony perspective'.

15. **On paradox:** Paradox is part of life and business. Understand it (as opposed to trying to resolve it), work with it, and learn from it. Examples of some of the paradoxical forces at work would include: global versus local, big versus small, relational versus technological (for some this represents a paradox, but for a younger generation it isn't), centralized versus decentralized. Contemporary leaders are required to lead in a world of paradox. Your only defence in such a context is to arm yourself with frameworks that will allow you to understand the paradox at play. Generational theory would be a good example of such a framework. It doesn't answer every question, but it does provide some profound insights as to the generational paradoxes you will encounter within your professional (and personal) environments.

16. **On adaptability:** Business growth comes about not through planning but through adapting. Adapting becomes the new way of living and of changing. In a predictable, ordered world, planning was possible. No longer is this the case given the systemic nature of the world in which we do business. Systems theory holds that the more complex the system, the less predictable it becomes. Delete (or perhaps shred) the elaborate plans that stretch beyond even where the *Starship Enterprise* has ventured and rather focus on ensuring that the inherent capacity for adaptation is imprinted throughout your business.

17. **On collaboration:** In a relational and networked world, leadership is no longer about control but rather about collaboration. This, of course, is far from simple, but there is a lot being said, studied, and written about the need for collaboration and it is something that 'won't go away'. Expect to see more on this subject and expect the 'volume to get louder'! Leaders need to understand that influence is now the new frontier of leadership. Thanks to the reality of social technologies, leaders can no longer expect to control the conversation. However, you can and must influence the conversations taking place that are of concern to you.

18. **On participation:** Create ownership at every level. Make a note of this point. Write it someplace where it will shout at you daily. Look at it and think about how you can do it. Invitational leadership suggests that it is a leader's responsibility to create the kind of environment that invites the best out of others. If those around you are not delivering their best, invitational leadership suggests that the blame starts with the leader!

19. **On diversity:** Embrace it! Diversity is the soil from which the twin challenges of (healthy) conflict and innovation will grow

and flourish. Research shows that diversity leads to resilience, and what leader would not want a resilient company? However, leading diversity is easier said than done. TomorrowToday Global, in conjunction with a leading international business school, has developed a day programme on leading diversity, and is scheduled for programmes located in both Russia and Singapore in the near future. In essence, we need to learn how to move *from* being different from each other to being different *for* each other. This is the challenging road in the quest towards harnessing diversity.

20. **On curiosity:** It will be more important to remain curious than be certain. This means that success will emerge from failure and we will need to be willing to 'try a lot of stuff and keep what works' (as Jim Collins said in *Good to Great*). It was Joseph Campbell who wrote, 'Where you stumble, there your treasure lies.' Work environments need to become 'safe sandboxes' – places where experimentation and risk-taking are encouraged, places of sheer play.

What then are the questions you should be asking that will spark learning and curiosity? This will mean embracing the marginal, the fringe. This is where the future is. Physicist David Bohm once said: 'The ability to perceive or think differently is more important than the knowledge gained.' Smart leaders know where to find the fringe and how best to manage it in order to create change and stimulate progress.

Who represents 'the fringe' in your business? Contact them now and set up a time when you can take them for coffee and explore their thinking and ideas.

21. **On storytelling:** Stories matter. So do stories about stories. Smart leaders will increasingly be seen as the 'storytellers' within the organisations they lead. Stories inform life. They hold us together and keep us apart. We inhabit the great stories of our culture. We live through stories. We are lived by the stories of our people and place. Look for the stories! Next time you are in a bookstore, browse through the children's section or, if that is too difficult, then buy *Who Moved My Cheese?* and read that. We have used Dr Seuss's classic *Oh, the Places You'll Go!* in a leadership programme, and we once facilitated an entire strategy process using a story framework. Stories provide content; they give context; they bring about coherency; they foster and nurture connection and can be used as a catalyst for change.

In facing up to the demands of leadership, some, or several, of these points may represent 'foreign territory' for you. They may represent an agenda or a journey that will require bold exploration or creating a new set of reference points altogether. It involves learning (and maybe 'unlearning') a whole new language and new customs. Acquiring these navigation points and skills, unfamiliar as they may be, will ultimately determine whether or not companies heading for tomorrow will thrive, or forever be 'lost at sea'.

Go on, take Charlie Parker's advice... live it! You won't be sorry you did.

Conclusion

Your journey to a new approach to leadership has begun.

At the start of this book, we urged you to do a few things.

We suggested you keep a journal. If you did that, now would be a good time to go back through your own thoughts and highlight key learnings and insights, and extract a 'to-do' and a 'not-to-do' (or 'stop doing') list.

We suggested you read through the book slowly, taking time to reflect on each chapter and put into practice some of the practical suggestions we gave and the ideas that emerged from your own reflections. If you kept a journal, you should have captured these. If you did not, now would be a good time to do so. Use the table of contents at the beginning of the book to remind you of what you have learnt, and what you plan to do with what you have learnt.

We also encouraged you to make contact with us, sharing your stories, your questions, your answers, and your insights. We hope you'll do that soon.

To connect with us, please go to
http://www.tomorrowtodayglobal.com/liacw_book to find a list of ways to further the conversation, and some additional recommended materials.

At that webpage, you'll also find an updated list of suggestions for your next steps.

This book is only a start. Not just for you, but for us as well. We will keep learning and developing, and we'll keep looking for ways to provide resources to leaders like you. Please go to the website above and see what resources and support are available for you to successfully develop yourself as a leader, now that you've taken the first steps towards leading in a changing world.

Margaret Mead, the sociologist, once said: 'Never doubt that a small group of thoughtful, committed citizens can change the world; indeed, it's the only thing that ever has.' You and your team, infused with the right mindsets and skills about this changing world we live in, can be just such a small group. And we truly believe that your leadership of that group will make all the difference in a world that is just waiting to discover what it is to become.

So now go.

And lead.

About the Authors

Keith Coats

International leadership thinker who speaks to the shifts required of leaders and organisations in both their thinking and practice if they are to successfully navigate the future.

Keith works hard to ask the questions that aren't being asked and then, together with the TomorrowToday Global team, builds frameworks of understanding that illuminate insights into the specific area of focus – be that leadership, talent, disruption, diversity, and bringing out the best in those you lead. As a founding partner in TomorrowToday Global, Keith has the privilege to work and consult across multiple industries, and to present to multicultural audiences in a global context at both an executive and senior leadership level.

Keith is a published author and, at the request of the King of Sweden, did work with the Sweden Economic Forum. Business schools and institutions, including London Business School, Duke CE, Gordon Institute of Business Science, and the East-West Center in Hawaii, repeatedly request his input in their premier executive and senior leadership programmes globally. Keith has also helped clients, including the Bookings Institute (Washington), Boeing, Spar, and Old Mutual, design customised leadership development programmes.

keith@tomorrowtodayglobal.com
www.keithcoats.com

Graeme Codrington

Expert in tracking the disruptive forces that are shaping the future of work, with a passion for the intersection of technology, people, and organisational systems.

Working with the team at TomorrowToday Global, Graeme develops strategic insights into disruptive change and what organisations need to do to thrive in the near future. He has done so for nearly two decades.

Graeme helps his clients to harness the opportunities inherent in the disruptive changes we're all experiencing right now.

He custom-designs each engagement to ensure his clients get precisely what they need, from keynote presentations to leadership programmes and online resources.

Graeme's international experience and depth of knowledge make him highly relevant in today's rapidly evolving business world. Along with his formal qualifications (five degrees) and research credentials (a number of research awards and four best-selling books), he has a wide range of business experience (he worked for KPMG, was involved in an IT startup, and is now a successful entrepreneur).

graeme@tomorrowtodayglobal.com
www.graemecodrington.com

Acknowledgements

We would like to thank our team at TomorrowToday Global – not just the current team at the time of writing this book, but all of the people who have been part of our journey over the past decade. Your insights, shared experiences, support, challenges, and professionalism have all been instrumental in shaping our understanding of the changing world and leadership. This book would not have been possible without you.

Keith would especially like to thank the many leaders who have sometimes unwittingly contributed significantly to my own leadership thinking and practice. Special mention must be made of my '3 Wise Men' – my mentors and friends Frank Luckin, Andrew McLean, and Dudley Forde. Your wisdom, generosity, example, and patience have been an invaluable gift along the journey. Thank you. Then, of course, there are those 'closer to home'. My business partners and colleagues, especially Graeme, without whom this journey simply would not have been possible; my children (and their partners) Keegan (Quinn), Tamryn (Geoff), and Sipho (who prefers the tag 'Daniel'), from whom I have – and continue to – learn so much; and then last but certainly not least, my amazing (and long suffering) wife, Vicky: the central force around whom I and our family orbit! Thank you.

Acknowledgements from Graeme: Nearly 25 years ago, as I was finishing formal studies in youth work, I was told to apply for a job at one of South Africa's largest and most successful youth organisations. That's when I met Keith Coats, the leader of that amazing organisation. In every way he epitomized the type of person I believed a changing world needed. And if you've ever met him in person, you will know Keith has that undefinable quality of presence. Quiet, self-effacing, introverted, and thoughtful, he can nevertheless dominate a room just by being there.

I will be forever grateful that Keith did not offer me the job I had applied for, instead gently guiding me onto another path. At that stage, neither of us knew that my new path and his would intersect again a few years later and eventually lead us to start our company, TomorrowToday Global, together. I did know from the first day I met him, though, that I wanted to stay connected to Keith, and to have him share my life's journey. He has done more than that – he has shaped it too. And I am privileged and honoured to now call him a friend as well. Maybe effusively praising one's co-author is not the most appropriate thing to do in a book's acknowledgement section. But in this case, it is well deserved.

So, to Keith: my friend, my business partner, my mentor (and sometimes my student – especially on technology issues), my sporting buddy and betting partner, and, yes, just a little bit, my hero – thanks. This book would not be possible without you. Because this book has taken over 20 years to write – 20 years spent together. And the best part of it for me is that it feels like we've only just begun.

One of the most important lessons one can learn in leadership is that it always happens in a context. Leadership is learnt by doing it and by being there. So, thank you to everyone who has allowed me to 'do it and be there', and in doing so, understand more deeply what leadership is. To my family, my friends, my colleagues, my clients, my faith community, and even the tribe who hangs out with me on social media and my critics: thank you all for shaping me into who I am, and for being the context in which I am able to learn to be the best version of me that I can be.

And, finally, from Keith and myself, thanks to Jude Foulston for making sure this book actually saw the light of day. Thanks, Jude, for nagging just enough, but not too much. And for everything else. Wind beneath wings. Light in the fog.

About TomorrowToday Global

We live and work in turbulent times of disruptive change. Merely improving on past successes is no longer a guarantee of business success. Your leaders and teams need to understand what is changing – and why – and adapt to new rules for success and failure. This requires shifts in mindset, attitudes, habits, and skills.

TomorrowToday's team of experts can assist in developing *your* leaders and teams by helping them understand the forces that are shaping the new world of work.

We work alongside you to provide strategic insights into the disruptive forces shaping the world right now. By doing so, we show you how to adapt and deal with constant change, assist you with personal and team development, and raise your organisation's confidence and creativity to successfully deliver on your strategies.

Our insights into the changing world of work are packaged in easily accessible formats, from presentations and workshops to online courses and extended leadership development programmes, all designed to drive real mindset and behaviour change through your organisation.

Our style is to combine well-researched strategic insights with common-sense wisdom, all laced with a gently rebuking humour and enlivened by multimedia and visually stunning presentations. We work hard to help you and your team to see 'tomorrow's world today', and to know how you need to think and act differently in the future.

If you want to be part of the new breed of leaders and have recognised that your business needs to change, but you are not sure what this change looks like or how to communicate it, then contact us on info@tomorrowtodayglobal.com as we'd love to work with you.

Other Books by the Authors:

Mind the Gap: *Understanding different generations: own your past, know your generation, choose your future (Graeme Codrington)*

Mind the Gap is for you if you want to know why: your 18-year-old son isn't interested in being a doctor – he wants to save the whale; your grandfather gives you Big Band CDs for your birthday; your secretary knows more than you do; your grandson calls you Peter instead of granddad. In short, this title aims to promote understanding between the generations. This is vitally important in all of our relationships, especially in the workplace.

Application chapters focus attention on: work, marketing and advertising, leadership, teamwork, finances, parenting, education and training, 're-tyrement', travel, politics, faith, health, and home. Still a best-selling book, with five-star reviews!

Future-proof Your Child for the 2020s and Beyond: *How to parent in disruptive times (Graeme Codrington)*

'Mommy, Daddy, what should I be when I grow up?' This is the question every child asks when they begin to develop a sense of the future, and it's never been harder for parents to answer it than now.

This century is characterised by disruptive change that is turning our world upside down. Jobs aren't just changing, but whole industries are ceasing to exist. The scripts for success and failure are being rewritten on a daily basis in our families, at work and in life. Do parents know who and what their children need to be, let alone what they might be able to do, in the future world of work?

This book doesn't just paint a picture of what the future might hold, but provides frameworks and practical advice for what parents can do today in order to build solid foundations for their children so as to maximise their chances of success. Children who are equipped with the right sets of skills, attitudes, and worldviews will remain relevant and able to take advantage of future opportunities.

Future-proof Your Child for the 2020s and Beyond is an invaluable guide for parents who wish to create realistic and relevant parenting goals that will set their children up to thrive, no matter what awaits them in the future.

Everything I Know about Leadership I Learnt from the Kids:
Leadership lessons from unlikely sources, with great discussion starters for teams and leaders (Keith Coats)

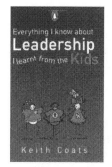

'Can I drive the car?' is a familiar refrain for most parents. But in dealing with this issue of control, trust, and training, is there a lesson to be learnt, a lesson that can be applied by leaders in the business environment?

Keith Coats has written a title that draws on everyday events in the life of his family, pointing out how these experiences translate into important lessons in leadership. Whether they are issues of control or communication, inspiration or loyalty, or simply getting through the tough times, Coats explores the universal lessons we learn as parents and shows how to apply them in the boardroom, the office, or the factory.

Made in United States
Orlando, FL
22 July 2024

49421329R00115